Profiles in Evangelism

Profiles in Evangelism

Biographical Sketches of World-Renowned Soul Winners

Fred Barlow

SWORD of the LORD
PUBLISHERS
P.O. BOX 1099, MURFREESBORO, TN 37133

Copyright, 1976
Sword of the Lord Publishers

ISBN 0-87398-659-8

SINCEREST APPRECIATION IS EXTENDED
TO BIBLICAL EVANGELISM FOR THE USE OF
THESE PROFILES WHICH WERE FIRST
PUBLISHED IN THE PAGES OF *THE BIBLICAL
EVANGELIST.*

Printed and bound in the United States of America

DEDICATION

Jacqueline Lou, Carolyn Louise, Gwendolyn Kay, Frederick William (Rick)—my four preacher's kids—gifts from God: because your consistent Christian testimony, concerned and compassionate interest and intercession for me and my ministry have been a source of strength as well as an inspiration in the family and out in the field of service for our Saviour, I gratefully dedicate this volume to you with the prayer that each of you will be counted by Christ to be winning worthies in the great work of evangelizing the unsaved.

Introduction

It is altogether appropriate in this bicentennial year of America's history that the story of some of its spiritual sons be published. Not every man mentioned is an American, but even so, each left a legacy whose influence and impact has been used of God for good across the two centuries of America's history.

These are short biographical sketches of men: men who did the work of an evangelist (II Tim. 4:5), that high, holy office, the individuals of which are a gift of God to the churches, to the nation (Eph. 4:11, 12)! As such, these worthies wrought revivals of righteousness, raised up standards of spirituality, resisted the forces of evil, redeemed through their preaching multitudes of death-doomed, Hell-bound sinners to Christ, to heavenly home and hope.

You will meet 46 of these soul-winning worthies in these pages. They are converts to Christ from the gold coast and the gutter, from Sunday schools, sawdust trails, skid rows; one was a sidewalk recruit. They come from the environments of a gypsy wagon, a rancher's home, parsonages, infidelism, Jewry, baseball diamond, the brothels, courts of law, the classroom, coal mines, cobbler's shop. They evangelized in the forest, in the field, from the pulpit, through the printed page, publicly, privately, in the arenas and from house to house.

Meet them in their hours of deepest conviction of sin, in the hallowed hours of their conversion of soul, in the holy hour of their call to evangelism, and in their hallelujah hours of conquests for Christ. Come walk with them, weep with them, warn the lost with them and win with them.

I trust these vignettes will be vital and valuable. They are penned with a purpose: to enlist, to enthuse, to encourage a host of readers to engage in the worthy work of evangelism!

1976   **Fred M. Barlow**

Table of Contents

Charles M. Alexander 9
Hyman J. Appelman 13
Francis Asbury 19
William Edward Biederwolf. 23
William Booth 27
David Brainerd 33
Billy Bray 36
Fred Brown, D.D. 41
E. Howard Cadle 45
William Carey 51
John Carrara 55
Peter Cartwright 61
J. Wilbur Chapman 65
Jonathan Edwards 69
Christmas Evans 73
Charles Grandison Finney .. 77
Mordecai Ham 82
"Praying Hyde" 87
Dr. Bob Jones, Sr. 93
Sam Jones 97
Adoniram Judson 103
Jacob Knapp 107
B. R. Lakin 111

Paul Levin 117
Robert Moffat 121
Dwight Lyman Moody 125
Henry C. Morrison 129
Asahel Nettleton 133
Sam Raborn 137
Bill Rice 143
John R. Rice 147
Evan Roberts 150
Ira David Sankey 155
Girolamo Savonarola 158
Lee R. Scarborough 163
Gipsy Smith 167
Charles Haddon Spurgeon . 171
Billy Sunday 175
T. DeWitt Talmage 181
J. Hudson Taylor 185
Reuben Archer Torrey 191
Mel Trotter 195
Dr. George W. Truett 199
"Uncle John" Vassar 203
John Wesley 207
George Whitefield 211

Charles M. Alexander

Charles M. Alexander

"Prince of Gospel Singers"

(1867-1920)

There was nothing two-faced about Charles McCallon Alexander, but one is surely safe is saying that this great gospel musician had a two-faceted ministry in evangelism and that he excelled in them both. Acknowledged to be the successor to Ira D. Sankey, and in some respects his superior, "Alexander was undoubtedly the greatest song leader and choir conductor of his time, and perhaps all time." But Charles Alexander was more than merely the "Prince of Gospel Singers," he was pre-eminently known in his day also as a soul winner—a powerful, fruitful, peerless personal worker!

In fact, Alexander achieved a record few full-time evangelists have ever experienced—he traveled twice around the world in search of souls. As one of his biographers, Dr. T. B. Davis, defined it:

> The Apostle Paul toured much of the world in his day, but it was only a portion of our planet. Whitefield and the two Wesleys, and Moody and Sankey visited America and England in their wonderful missions for the salvation of the lost; but it remained for Dr. Reuben A. Torrey and Mr. Charles M. Alexander completely to circle the globe, and then for Mr. Alexander to make a second trip, revisiting old scenes, leading thousands in gospel song and preaching Christ to individuals on land and sea.

Both tours were successes. In the first tour, over 100,000 people made public professions of Christ, and many were led to Christ personally and in his preaching missions on the second tour.

Alexander's purpose and passion for soul winning were

PROFILES IN EVANGELISM

brought about by his father's death in 1890. Until that time, Charles, converted to Christ in a devout Presbyterian home in Tennessee at thirteen, was content to be a good Christian and teach music at nearby Maryville Academy and college. But his father's death shocked him "into serious re-examination of his life's direction and ambitions." And, as Dr. Faris Whitesell wrote: *"He was impressed with the hollowness of all else except the work of Christ, so he dedicated himself to full-time Christian service. . .with a deep yearning to bring souls to Christ."*

Resigning his academy position, he helped a Quaker evangelist for a short season, then enrolled in Moody Bible Institute. After graduation, he assisted Evangelist M. B. Williams in midwest campaigns for eight years. Then Dr. Torrey invited him to assist him in the music for his 1902-1908 globe-girdling campaigns.

Alexander became famous overnight as a result of the Australia crusade (first stop on the tour). His conducting captivated and controlled the great crowds of tens of thousands and brought forth such singing as had never been heard in Australian cities. (The same could be said of American, British Isles, Ceylon cities, too.) It was in Melbourne that Alexander introduced the "Glory Song" ("That Will Be Glory" by Charles Gabriel), which swept like a fire across the cities and continent and prompted one writer to witness, "set Australia on fire."

Alexander led the congregations like a great choir, drilling them with "the decision and authority of a first-class drill sergeant." He scolded, rebuked, exhorted, jested. "And the great audiences enjoyed it." They sang "with ease and fire and exultation" to the magnetic man, with waving arms for a baton, with expressive radiant face and fine voice. "And the note of triumphant faith that ran through it all, melted the audience as fire melted wax." Alexander's music fulfilled its highest function of preparing the congregation for the preacher and his message.

Alexander was not only a master of music, he also excelled in personal evangelism. "He led everyone of his special helpers, not already a Christian, to Christ—his pianists, soloists, and secretaries." Noteworthy among those professions was the conversion of Robert Harkness, a self-righteous musical genius who was saved under the patient, persistent efforts of Alexander. Today's hymnals have many of Harkness' compositions: "He Will Hold Me Fast," "Is He Yours?" etc.

Alexander was not only a successful soul winner, "he had the unusual ability to enlist others in the work of soul winning." One of his biographers, Dr. T. B. Davis, was literally "pushed" into soul winning by Alexander. Davis, a syndicated religious newspaper reporter, was studying the crowd during an invitation, seeking some incident to write up. The altar was full and the workers insufficient. Seeing Davis, Alexander asked, "What are you doing here, Davis, while people are down there waiting to be led to Christ?"

"I'm watching for an incident for my articles," was the reply.

"Get off the platform and lead some of those people to Christ and you'll have some firsthand incidents to tell," and a firm, gentle push accompanied his words.

In this act, Alexander was simply insisting on what he preached: "You claim you are following Jesus. Are you fishing for men? If you are not fishing, you are not following."

Alexander practiced what he preached. His wife, the former Helen Cadbury—of the Birmingham, England, cocoa family and fame—said of him: "To Charles Alexander, every new soul with whom he came in contact thrilled him with an ardor as fresh as if it were the first with whom he came in contact to lead to Jesus." Thus the great platform man witnessed, warned and won the lost to Christ—in meetings, yes, but also on the streets (in Melbourne he walked the streets a whole night seeking to win a man to Christ; in hospitals (he led two of the nurses to Christ after an appendectomy); in restaurants, cabs—anywhere and everywhere!

Alexander died at fifty-three years of age, but, as Dr. Whitesell commented, "The last thirty of those years were so rich in soul winning that their fruitage will abide forever." Aye, put it down: Charles Alexander—the great gospel musician—but, even greater, a prince among personal workers! *May many more musicians follow in his train!*

Hyman J. Appelman

Evangelist

(1902-1983)

The first time I sat under the eloquent and fervent ministry of Evangelist Hyman Appelman, I felt I was listening to a man of God with a ministry and a message akin to that of the apostles of the first century! I find I have not been alone in that thought because testimonials by many men of God to this worldwide honored evangelist have echoed the same sentiment.

Dr. R. G. Lee wrote these lines: "In loyalty to the Bible, in spiritual fervor in seeking the lost for Christ, in effectual preaching of the Gospel with spiritual passion. . .at all places and before all congregations, he is God's faithful ambassador."

Dr. Lee Roberson wrote: *"The first time that I listened to him preach my heart was stirred by his fervor, zeal, and passion for souls. . .for thirty-five years there has been no abatement of his zeal and his concern for the souls of men."*

Dr. W. Herschel Ford said, "Men of all races have heard the Gospel from your lips. You have been able to walk with kings, but you have not lost the common touch. . . .You have sought the Lord's face and you have brought the world a message from His great heart."

I first heard Dr. Appelman when I was in the first years of my ministry as a Bible college graduate. In those mid-forties, evangelism was at a low ebb in America. Evangelists were considered to be charlatans, religious quacks, money-hungry. Spirituality was in a sad state. Churches were deserted, Christians defeated, the Lord's

Hyman J. Appelman

day desecrated, Christ was dethroned, fundamentalism degraded, revival campaigns despised.

But God raised up some mighty men to motivate and move old-time evangelism back into power and pre-eminence. *Hyman Appelman was one of those men!* Small wonder, then, that this writer, seated night after night in that Akron, Ohio, Appelman crusade, witnessing increasing attendances, deepening conviction, miraculous conversions, revival fires being lighted under powerful, pungent preaching, felt he was listening to apostolic ministry. Suffice it to say, that campaign was one of the historic, highlight events in molding my ministry. I shall always be indebted to God for it.

Appelman was born of Jewish parents in Moghiliev, White Russia, January 7, 1902. At the age of twelve he emigrated to Chicago where he studied law and received his degree from DePaul University. His legal ability is evidenced in his evangelism for Appelman preaches a clear, analytical and authoritative message, presenting his case with pleading appeals to his audiences to confess sin, crown Christ King and be converted.

On March 19, 1925, Appelman was converted to Christ himself. In the study of Dr. James E. Davis, pastor of Central Christian Church, Denver, Colorado, Appelman called upon the name of the Lord Jesus. "It was a culmination of a conscious lifetime search for inner peace and satisfaction," Appelman relates. He further cites, "Before then I was an orthodox Jew living up to the Judaistic religion as much as I could. I always believed in God, in the Old Testament, in a resurrection, a judgment, a Heaven and a Hell. All Dr. Davis had to do was to show me that Jesus of Bethlehem-Nazareth was the promised Messiah—was more than a man—that He died and rose again."

After his conversion, Appelman believed he was called to preach. However, it was five years later that he fully surrendered and went to Southwestern Baptist Seminary, Fort Worth, Texas, to prepare to preach. After graduation, Appelman became a pastor, ministering in half-time and

16 *PROFILES IN EVANGELISM*

full-time churches in Oklahoma and Texas. In 1934 he accepted the position of state evangelist with the Texas Baptist Convention (Southern), a position he held until 1942.

January of that year Hyman Appelman led in the "Christ for Philadelphia Evangelistic Crusade," the campaign that commenced the present-day era of union, citywide campaigns in America. Twenty-seven hundred professions of faith were recorded in that eighteen-day Philadelphia crusade. Then it was Los Angeles, Detroit, Akron; aye, across the nation in almost every state. In every one of those campaigns Appelman estimates there were over one thousand professions of faith in Christ, some of the campaigns approximating 2,500 to 3,000 such decisions.

His ministry has now carried him worldwide—Australia in 1949: 8,600 professions in six months; British Isles—1951: 1,400 professions in twelve weeks; Kerala and Madera states (India)—5,893 professions in three months.

In recent years Dr. Appelman has conducted not only citywide, but also local church campaigns; yes, even brush-arbor meetings! In fact, it was under a brush arbor in Hill County, Texas, that Appelman experienced the first great display of God's power in his ministry. That was back in 1930. Many are the men, women and youth who have made decisions for the Saviour since those days. For the statistically minded, Dr. Appelman estimates over 445,000 decisions in his ministry of thirty-five years, with over 270,000 uniting with the churches, hundreds surrendering for full-time service, and multiplied other thousands rededicating lives to the Lord. He attributes these phenomenal figures, the Christ-honoring revival victories under God, to *"prayer-soaked, organized preparation and promotion and cooperation, a little by the evangelist, much by the pastors and churches."*

Appelman is of the old school that believes "the primal requisites of every revival are found, among other places, in I Samuel 7:3; Psalm 85:6; Acts 4:31-33; in a general concern for the presence of the Lord, an earnest attention to the

Word of the Lord, a sincere renunciation of sin against the Lord, a public dedication to the service of the Lord—without these there can be *no revival! With them revival is assured!"*

And Appelman encourages all in the fact that revival is possible in our swinging, sinning, sophisticated seventies. His formula?

> Revival will come today when enough of us go back—back to Pentecost, back to the book of Acts, back to the Upper Room of prayer, back to the tarrying commanded by the Lord for Holy Ghost power, back to restudy, reanalyze, realign ourselves and our churches to the program of the apostolic days, when with nothing but surrendered lives filled with the Holy Spirit to show the world, twelve apostles, one hundred and twenty disciples, five hundred followers of the lowly Nazarene, rose from their knees fire-baptized, going forth to preach the Gospel that changed the world and keeps on changing it for God, for men, for time, for Eternity.

As I said earlier, when you hear Dr. Hyman Appelman, you feel you are listening to a man of God with a message and a ministry akin to that of the apostles of the first century!

Francis Asbury

Frontier Bishop

(1745-1816)

One Labor Day I attended some special services sponsored by the Chicago-area Regular Baptist churches and held in an old Methodist camp-meeting ground in Des Plaines. I confess that as I listened to some great preaching that day, I also looked around that rustic, multi-sided, sawdust-floored tabernacle and allowed my mind to wander back two centuries and imagined that I was in attendance at an old-time Methodist camp-meeting, listening to a Francis Asbury.

Those were the days when Methodist men were men of might, and the slight-built, five-foot six inches-in-height, one-hundred and fifty pounds-in-weight Asbury was one of the mightiest of the Methodists. And nowhere was this powerful preacher more at home than in a camp meeting. *"The camp meetings appealed to Francis because of their fervor and the enthusiasm with which his preaching was greeted. He discovered there was an evangelistic eagerness in these forests which found an answering response in his own heart. . . ."* In his *Journal* Francis painted a vivid picture of the gathering, writing, "The stand was in the open air, embosomed in a wood of lofty beech trees. Fires, blazing here and there, dispelled the darkness; and the shouts of the redeemed captives and the cries of the precious souls, struggling into life, broke the silence of midnight."

Unbelievably, those lines were written by a *bishop*. But Asbury, appointed by John Wesley to become his "general

20 *PROFILES IN EVANGELISM*

assistant" in America, and ordained a bishop of the Methodist church thirteen years after his arrival in America from his native England, was no ordinary bishop.

Asbury remained a circuit-riding preacher all of his forty-five years in the ministry. He was the sort of a bishop who was never addressed as "my Lord; having no splendid palace, no magnificent cathedral, no snug diocese; separating himself from all the comforts of life for sixty dollars a YEAR, plunging into the wilderness to seek for lost sheep, preaching in barns, on stumps of trees scorched by suns, bitten by driving snows, swimming vast rivers."

In those forty-five years, Asbury recorded that he rode the "lonely road" (as Methodists delight to call it) one hundred and seventy-five thousand miles by horse, and twenty-five thousand more miles in a carriage when he became too infirm to ride horseback. Yet with all that tiresome travel, Asbury preached twenty thousand sermons.

Asbury, more than any one man, was synonomous with the success of early Methodism in America. He was Methodism personified and he was the pulse, the power that propelled its ministry across the colonies. When he arrived in America, October 27, 1771, there were less than eighty preachers and fourteen thousand members in Methodism. When he died there were about two hundred thousand members, two thousand local pastors, and from "eighty to five hundred itinerant preachers." America in that day had about five million population and it is estimated that Methodists were reaching two million of them—*nearly one half of the people!*

This was not accomplished without personal price by Asbury and his associates. Pioneer life was a painstaking lot, but traveling for a preacher was often perilous, usually entailed privations, and many problems. Writing in his *Journal* in 1803, Asbury recorded:

> No room to retire to; that in which you sit is common to all, crowded with women and children; the fire occupied with cooking; much and long-loved solitude not to be found, unless you choose to run out in the woods in the

Francis Asbury 21

rain. Six months in the year, I have had, for thirty-two years, occasionally submitted to what will never be agreeable to me; but the people, it must be confessed, are among the kindest in the world. But kindness will never make a crowded log cabin, twelve feet by ten, agreeable; without are cold and rain, and within six adults and as many children, one of which is all motion; the dogs must sometimes be admitted.

In light of this itinerant life that would abbreviate any personal home life (Asbury estimated he would only be home one week a year) and in light of his meagre monies (some of which Asbury "administered to the necessities of a beloved mother until I was fifty-seven") Asbury never saw it right to marry. Thus he rode "the lonely road," Methodism's bishop on horseback!

Asbury had planned to return to England if God did not honor his labors in the new land, but He abundantly did as we have seen. When the Revolutionary War broke out and Wesley commanded all Englishmen to return, Asbury defied the order and dared the ridicule, the reproach and even possible death from the colonists who viewed every Englishman as a possible enemy. Asbury was shot at, imprisoned, and for a season sought refuge in more neutral Delaware, but he played the part of a shepherd, for he had insisted, "It would be an eternal dishonor to the Methodists that we should leave three thousand souls who desire to commit themselves to our care; neither is it the part of a good shepherd to leave his flock in danger: therefore, I am determined, by the grace of God, not to leave them, let the consequence be what it may."

That determinate spirit of Asbury was the same that prompted him to pen on his voyage to America: "I will set down a few things that lie on my mind. Whither am I going? To the new world. What to do? To gain honor? No, not if I know my own heart. To get money? No; I am going to live to God, and to bring others so to do."

No idle boast, that affirmation of Asbury! For until he laid down his life near Fredericksburg, Virginia, March 31, 1816, Asbury spent and was spent in seeking sinners for the

PROFILES IN EVANGELISM

Saviour and seeking to do the will of God. As Dr. Norman Nygaard noted:

> So finally came to rest in the country of his adoption. . .a man who, in his own lifetime, had been responsible for the founding of a great evangelical movement, and later a church, in America, who planted the cross of Christ in hamlets and countryside of the wilderness, and who gave to the land. . .a sturdy pioneer faith which molded to a tremendous degree not only the Methodist church but the religious faith of all of America.

In that Methodist campground on Labor Day, and at my desk today, I find myself praying to God for our America in our day: desperate, dark, degenerate, doom-destined day: Lord, send us some similar men, men that should make up the hedge, and stand in the gap before You for the land, that You should not destroy it. Amen!

William Edward Biederwolf

Evangelist

(1867-1934)

Presbyterians produced some of the most noteworthy evangelists of the late 1800's and early 1900's—and a noteable among them was William E. Biederwolf. Hoosier-born, (Monticello, Indiana, September 29, 1867), Biederwolf was content to be a Hoosier schoolmaster until his conversion to Christ. Revival meetings were on in the Monticello Presbyterian Church. Some of his closest friends accepted Christ and, getting concerned about "Ed," they drove a buggy to his boarding house twenty miles out in the country to invite him home for the weekend. It was a welcome invitation for a country schoolteacher and Biederwolf accepted. The result—*Sunday night he was saved!* Paraphrasing his own words:

His sins seemed to be falling upon him like a crushing mountain.

He saw Calvary and the Son of God lifted up on that cross and realized it was for him.

That conviction, coupled with the prayers and saintly life of his mother and a devoted sister, "all began surging about and beating against the door of his troubled soul"—and at the sermon's conclusion Biederwolf fell to his knees to call on Christ for cleansing and conversion. He soon went to college, continuing his education at Princeton, Erlangen and Berlin universities, and at the Sorbonne in Paris.

Ironically enough, Biederwolf's first church was the Broadway Presbyterian Church of Logansport, Indiana. It

William Edward Biederwolf

William Edward Biederwolf

was there, as a "dusty, tired, hungry runaway high school boy," he had once sat upon its steps to rest awhile! He became a chaplain in the Spanish-American War and then entered evangelism—a ministry he was to serve for thirty-five years.

Biederwolf's evangelism was nationwide and worldwide. Three times he circled the world in a soul-winning ministry. Perhaps his greatest foreign success was in 1924, when his team toured the principal cities of Japan, China, Korea, the Philippines, Siam, India and Australia!

In America he ministered from coast to coast. And in conjunction with his evangelism, Dr. Biederwolf was associated with the world-renowned Winona Lake Bible Conference for forty years. Twenty of those years he was director of the conference and was also instrumental in organizing the Winona Lake School of Theology. Biederwolf, sensing the fearful failure of family worship in American homes in his day, also founded the Family Altar League. At his death, it was estimated that over 250,000 family altars had been started. In 1929, Biederwolf became pastor of the storied Royal Poinciana Chapel in Palm Beach, Florida, a position he held until his death in 1934.

Biederwolf's ministry was mighty. Doubtlessly his greatest campaign was conducted in Oil City, Pennsylvania, in the bitter winter of 1914. Thousands thronged the tabernacle. Twice it was enlarged. Sinners came nightly to "seek the saving touch of the hand of God's Christ." Biederwolf's preaching was no shallow, skim-milk, simply-a-collection-of-stories-spun-around-a-Scripture-passage kind of preaching. His messages were pungent, powerful presentations of what Biederwolf insisted and proved: *"that the most successful revival finds its inspiration and power in the preaching of the essential, the fundamental, the trenchant doctrines of the Word of God."*

I have some of his books of sermons. Some of the titles in his book, *Evangelistic Sermons*, read thusly: "The Deity of Christ," "The Incarnation of Christ," "The Atonement," "The Resurrection," "The Second Coming,"

"Repentance," "The New Birth," "Hell," "Heaven," etc. It was this kind of preaching that brought *"men and women from every walk in life coming in deep contrition for their sins, the mayor of the city, physicians, lawyers, and men from the factories, young people from the schools, and the whole city and county were mightily stirred in deep concern about the things of God."*

Suffice it to say, our sin-soaked, sin-sated, death-doomed and Hell-bound Twentieth-Century society needs the same kind of Scripture-saturated, sin-rebuking, Christ-exalting, soul-winning-emphasizing preaching that Biederwolf practiced and won with all across our country in his day. May we not be guilty of watering down our message today to the siren calls of convenience and ecumenicity in evangelism! Our needs are too pressing and too paramount.

William Booth

Salvationist

(1829-1912)

"Pawnbroker to Pulpit!" William Booth could have used that subject any time he gave his life story in a revival crusade. When just a youth, he was taken out of school to become an apprentice pawnbroker in his native Nottingham, England, and he later plied the pawnbroker's trade in London's seamy south suburb of Walworth. Doubtlessly, it was in this environment where he saw the wretchedness, the poverty, the depravity and misery of the masses that Booth's heart felt its first hunger to help a fallen humanity.

Five months after Booth began his apprenticeship, an epochal event occurred which, too, was to shape his soul toward the spiritual—he was rudely awakened from his sleep to see his father die. It was the scene of a death-bed "repentance," for it was "the first time in his life Samuel Booth professed any interest in religion." As he died—with an Anglican minister, William's mother, and his two sisters singing "Rock of Ages"—an indelible impression was made upon the soul of the young Booth. He began attending Broad Street Wesleyan Chapel and once, after hearing a disturbing discourse on "A Soul Dies Every Minute," and reflecting on his sins, young William Booth "publicly repented and made the surrender of his soul to God. Instantly the burden of his guilt was rolled away, his soul was flooded with peace, and from that hour it was his fixed purpose to devote himself to God and to his generation."

He was fifteen and, at first, young Booth plunged into

William Booth

William Booth

politics—*revolutionary* politics. He was appalled by the awful crying of children begging bread, outraged by the fathers who pawned their last possession for one more drink, and inflamed by "the passionate oratory of the Chartist, Feargus O'Conner." But another man influenced Booth about the same time. Rev. James Caughey, an American revivalist, was used by God to challenge Booth to "proclaim the everlasting Gospel to others." And at seventeen years of age, William Booth preached his first sermon. Incredibly, in that first sermon in a cottage on Kidd Street, Booth preached some of the principles that would be practices of his future "Army."

He preached on street corners, still plying his trade as a pawnbroker. On Sundays he would round up his rag-tag, ragamuffin group of drunkards, wife-beaters, and bring them to the chapel, often leading many of them forward for prayer and penitence. But the elders of the chapel, repelled by the sight and stench of products of his street evangelism, expelled him from the membership. Booth had been sympathetic to the Reformers and joined them, but he soon wearied of their ways of making "hirelings" out of their preachers. However, it was during his short stay with the Reformers that young Booth met Catherine Mumford, the woman he would marry, and the woman who would be known worldwide as the "Mother of the Army."

Booth briefly considered the Congregationalists, but as he read thirty or forty pages of Abraham Booth's, *Reign of Grace*, which stressed the Calvinistic doctrine of election, Booth was so repelled "he threw the book across the room, resolved to have nothing to do with it." He then fellowshiped with the Methodist New Connection, carrying on evangelistic work under their sponsorship. He soon chafed under the submission to their authority and, in 1857, entered evangelism as an independent.

It was in a tent campaign in London's Whitechapel area, Booth heard and heeded the call that would result in his worldwide work. Coming home one night, he greeted his wife,

30   PROFILES IN EVANGELISM

Oh, Kate, I have found my destiny. These are the people for whose salvation I have been longing all these years. As I passed the doors of the flaming sin-palaces tonight I seemed to hear a voice sounding in my ears, "Where can you go and find such heathen as these, and where is there so great a need for your labours?" And there and then in my soul I offered up myself and you and the children to this great work. These people shall be our people, and they shall have our God for their God.

Booth preached in that tent and, when winter weather came, in an old dancing hall. Then a house was purchased, a theater rented, even a pigeon shop and a skittle-alley housed their meetings. The East London Christian Mission, as it was known, attracted great crowds and resulted in hosts of converts. But Booth knew the work needed some permanency of place if it were to survive. Again God raised up a man to minister to Booth's financial needs. A Mr. Edward Raymond Rabbits, a bootmaker, a Reformer, had subsidized Booth so he could make the transition from a pawnbroker to a full-time preacher. At Whitechapel it was a Mr. Morey and a Mr. Reed who gave great financial assistance to help the struggling ministry and the needy family of ten.

Thus in 1869 the Christian Mission was on firm financial ground: there were 14 preaching stations, some soup kitchens, 140 services indoors and outdoors each week. By now Mrs. Booth was preaching, too, a most unheard of precedent in preaching.

In 1878, the Mission received its new name—"Salvation Army." Probably a convert, Lijah Cadman, prompted the title, although Catherine is credited with it, too. The organization already had its "Rules and Regulations." Advertising often announced, "War! War! 2,000 men and women wanted to join the Hallelujah Army!" In 1878 a copy of the Mission magazine announced that the mission had "organized a salvation army to carry the blood of Christ and the fire of the Holy Spirit into every corner of the world." From there transitions were made easily and effortlessly: the General Superintendent became the "General," members became "Soldiers," evangelists

William Booth 31

became "Officers," uniforms were adopted. Services were held in "barracks" later called "citadels." Brass bands were begun and military terms instituted. A flag was designed and the motto, "Blood and Fire," adopted. In 1880 the official magazine became the *War Cry.*

The charter of the Army was to carry "the blood of Christ and fire of the Holy Ghost into every corner of the world." The United States was the first nation to be "invaded." First it was Philadelphia, then New York City, then other citadels were organized. Australia was opened and, in 1881, Marichale, Booth's eldest daughter, began the work in France. When General Booth died in 1912, *"there were ministries in fifty-eight countries, the Gospel preached in thirty-four languages, a record unparalleled in the history of any other religious organization."*

Booth's ministry originally was exclusively evangelistic, but he determined that one could not preach religion to a man with an empty stomach. Thus he set out "to minister to the physical that the spiritual may be made the more effective." Josiah Strong spoke of his successes: "Probably during no one hundred years in the history of the world have there been saved so many thieves, gamblers, drunkards and prostitutes as during the past quarter of a century through the heroic faith and labors of the Salvation Army."

That success was not without price, persecution, imprisonments, beatings, bludgeonings, brickbats, etc. One well wrote, *"The early salvationists won with scars and bloody noses, the respect which was to assure toleration of their privilege."*

Something of the spirit of the "salvationists" in those days was the spirit of their founder. Even after blindness took one eye, and he "was worn out," Booth evangelized until his death. Something of the compelling constraint, the impelling motivation that moved him to tireless activity in soul winning is seen in these two episodes before royalty in his native England.

Queen Victoria called him in once to enquire, "General

PROFILES IN EVANGELISM

Booth, what is the secret of your ministry? How is it that others are so pale, so pallid, so powerless, so weak, and you are so mighty." William Booth looked into the face of his queen and, with tears streaming down his face that looked so much like an Elijah or a Moses, said, "Your Majesty, I guess the reason is because God has all there is of me. . . .I guess it is because God knows that I am hungering [to keep souls out of] Hell!"

And on June 24, 1904, William Booth wrote in the autograph album of King Edward VII:

"Some men's ambition is art,
Some men's ambition is fame,
Some men's ambition is gold
My ambition is the souls of men."

A wild, wierd, wicked world today needs some more men with the same heart-hunger!

David Brainerd

Missionary

(1718-1747)

By almost every standard known to modern missionary boards, David Brainerd would have been rejected as a missionary candidate. He was tubercular—*died of that disease at twenty-nine*—and from his youth was frail and sickly. He never finished college, being expelled from Yale for criticizing a professor and for his interest and attendance in meetings of the "New Lights," a religious organization. He was prone to be melancholy and despondent.

Yet this young man, who would have been considered a real risk by any present-day mission board, became a missionary to the American Indians and, in the most real sense, "the pioneer of modern missionary work." Brainerd began his ministry with the Indians in April, 1743, at Kannameek, New York, then ministered in Crossweeksung and Cranberry (near Newark), New Jersey. These were the areas of his greatest successes.

Brainerd's first journey to the Forks of the Delaware to reach that ferocious tribe resulted in a miracle of God that preserved his life and revered him among the Indians as a "Prophet of God." Encamped at the outskirts of the Indian settlement, Brainerd planned to enter the Indian community the next morning to preach to them the Gospel of Christ. Unknown to him, his every move was being watched by warriors who had been sent out to kill him. F. W. Boreham recorded the incident:

But when the braves drew closer to Brainerd's tent,

PROFILES IN EVANGELISM

> they saw the paleface on his knees. And as he prayed, suddenly a rattlesnake slipped to his side, lifted up its ugly head to strike, flicked its forked tongue almost in his face, and then without any apparent reason, glided swiftly away into the brushwood. "The Great Spirit is with the paleface!" the Indians said; and thus they accorded him a prophet's welcome.

That incident in Brainerd's ministry illustrates more than the many Divine interventions of God in his life—it also illustrates the importance and intensity of prayer in Brainerd's life. Believe it—Brainerd prayed! Read the *Life and Diary of David Brainerd*. On page after page one reads such sentences as:

> **Wednesday, April 21.** . . .and God again enabled me to wrestle for numbers of souls, and had much fervency in the sweet duty of intercession. . . .

> **Lord's Day, April 25.** This morning I spent about two hours in secret duties and was enabled more than ordinarily to agonize for immortal souls. Though it was early in the morning and the sun scarcely shined at all, yet my body was quite wet with sweat. . . .

> **Saturday, December 15.** Spent much time in prayer in the woods and seemed raised above the things of this world. . . .

> **Monday, March 14.** . . .in the morning was almost continually engaged in ejaculatory prayer. . . .

> **Thursday, August 4.** Was enabled to pray much, through the whole day. . . .

> **Thursday, November 3.** Spent this day in secret fasting, and prayer, from morning till night. . . .

Suffice it to say, it is not surprising to read then of the miraculous interventions of God on Brainerd's behalf, and of the mighty ministry and the unbelievable revivals he experienced among the iniquitous, idolatrous heathen Indians in those short years. A volume such as this prohibits more than only mere mention of some of those supernal, supernatural scenes: *"I have now baptized, in all, forty-seven persons of the Indians. Twenty-three adults and twenty-four children. . . .Through rich grace, none of them as yet have been left to disgrace their profession of*

Christianity by any scandalous or unbelieving behavior" (Nov. 20, 1743). What pastor or evangelist reading this can say the same?

> **Lord's Day, December 29.** . . .After public worship was over, I went to my house, proposing to preach again after a short season of intermission. But they soon came in one after another; with tears in their eyes, to know, "what they should do to be saved. . . ." It was an amazing season of power among them, and seemed as if God had "bowed the heavens and come down. . ." and that God was about to convert the whole world.

His *Diary* and *Journal* are abrim with ministries and miracles that were akin to the acts of the Apostles. The *Life and Diary of David Brainerd* ought to be read—and read often—by God's people. It will do something for you spiritually. You will be convicted, challenged, changed, charged. It has had life-transforming effect upon many, motivating them to become missionaries, evangelists, preachers, people of prayer and power with God.

Brainerd died in 1747 in the home of Jonathan Edwards. His ministry to the Indians was contemporary with Wesley, Whitefield and Edwards as they ministered to the English-speaking people during that period called in English and American history, the "Great Awakening." Brainerd's centuries-spanning influence for revival is positive proof God *can* and *will* use any vessel, no matter how fragile and frail, if it is only sold out to souls and the Saviour!

Billy Bray

Evangelist

(1794-1888)

He started out his life in the *gutter*. He ended it shouting his last word, *"Glory!"* That word became the word that welled up in his heart, burst as a paean of praise from his lips after his conversion to Christ—so much so, that on one occasion Billy Bray bragged, "If you shut me up in a barrel, I'll shout glory to God through the bunghole."

Yes, Billy Bray lived the glory-life after the salvation of his soul and everybody knew it by the praise from his lips and the purity and power of his life. Glory-life was the norm for this converted Cornish miner who confessed, "I can say *glory, glory,* I can sing *glory, glory.* I can dance *glory, glory,"* generally accompanying the last word with the act.

A dying Christian breathed to Billy "in a voice weakened to a whisper, 'I wish I had a voice, so that I might praise the Lord,' to which Billy quietly, but satirically stated, 'You should have praised Him, my brother, when you had one.' "

But Billy Bray was not always a "praising God, preaching Christ and pleading with sinners to be saved" person. The twelvetrees, Cornwall, England-born miner (June 1, 1794) wasted his early years in profligacy, profanity, pipe-smoking and drinking himself drunk. Profanity must be a weak word to describe Bray's blasphemies, for his wicked comrades testified of his terrible, fearful blasphemies "that his oaths must come from Hell, for they smelt of sulphur." And Bray was

Billy Bray 37

boasted of being the "wildest, most daring and reckless of all the reckless, daring men," and a defier of God!

But, doubtlessly, his deepest, direst and most disgusting depravities resulted from the Devil's drink. Bray recounted those days of dissolution and drunkenness:

> Turned away from the mine at which I worked, for being insolent to the captain, I removed to another part of Devonshire, and as if to make my damnation sure, went to live at a beer shop. There with other drunkards, I drank all night long. But I had a sore head and a sick stomach, and worse than all, horrors of mind that no tongue can tell. I used to dread to go to sleep for fear of waking up in Hell; and though I made many promises to the Lord to be better, I was soon as bad or worse than ever. After being absent from my native country seven years, I returned a DRUNKARD!

Twenty-nine years old, married (somehow his wife stayed with him through all his debauchery and drunkenness), Bray began reading Bunyan's *Visions of Heaven and Hell.* He was particularly smitten by the description of *"two lost souls in Hell cursing each other, for being the author of each other's misery, and that they who love one another on earth will hate one another in Hell."* One of Bray's best friends, *"to whom he was much attached, was also much attached to him. They worked together, and went to alehouse and got drunk together. The arrow that pierced his soul was the thought, 'Shall S. Coad and I, who like each other so much, torment each other in Hell!' "*

From that time "he set out to be a better man," but one morning in November, 1823, about three o'clock, Bray jumped out of bed, fell upon his knees and cried for mercy from the Lord. It appears he did not receive full assurance of salvation until a couple of days later, an experience Bray later explained,

> I said to the Lord, "Thou has said, 'They that ask receive, they that seek shall find, and to them that knock the door shall be opened,' and I have faith to believe it." In an instant the Lord made me so happy that I could not

PROFILES IN EVANGELISM

express what I felt. I shouted for joy. I praised God with my whole heart for what He had done for a poor sinner like me; for I could say, The Lord hath pardoned all my sins.

Bray was not only pardoned, he was transformed. He became a new creation in Christ: cleansed, converted and called to preach Christ and convert others. At the time, some said Bray was "mad," and others said that "they would get him back again next payday." But later Bray thrillingly told, "Praise the Lord, it is now more than forty years, and they have not got me yet. They said I was a *mad*-man, but they meant I was a *glad*-man, and, glory be to God—I have been glad ever since."

Right! For as one biographer wrote of Bray, "Religion to Billy was not a duty to be done—not a privilege to be enjoyed in leisure hours—not a benefit club, a comfortable position for 'rainy days'—it was a *life.*"

And what a life it was! He preached, he prayed, he raised money to build chapels, he took orphans into his home, he visited the sick, he exuded the joy and the love of the Lord.

Perhaps Bray was at his best for God in his prayer life, for, from the earliest hour of his conversion, he learned to pray the prayer of faith. Such sure, simple belief which "staggered not at the promise of God through unbelief" made him "happy and contented with his lot, saved him from all anxious care, and diffused all over the whole of his life a heavenly radiance, some of the rays which fell upon others wherever he went."

But he was also at his best as a witness for his Lord. Wrote a friend of Bray about him,

Billy was so completely absorbed with a desire to do good—so fired with a zeal for the honor of his Divine Master—so full of pity towards his fellow men. . .so impressed with a continual sense of God's favor and presence, that without regard to position, or rank, or character, or circumstances, he was ever ready to testify to the reality and blessedness of religion, or to administer such reproof, or counsel, or warning, as he deemed necessary.

Such a winning witness is seen in his last hours:

After the doctor examined him, Billy said, "Well, Doctor, how is it?" "You are going to die." Billy instantly shouted, "Glory to God. Glory to God. I shall soon be in Heaven." Then he added in a low tone, and in his own peculiar way, "When I get up there, shall I give them your compliments, Doctor, and tell them you are coming too?" *"This,"* the doctor said, *"made a wonderful impression on me."*

Friday, May 22, 1888, Billy went to that long Home. His last word was "glory." His was a life and death that occasioned one to say of that earnest evangelist, *"He was blessing and praising the Lord all the day, so that Heaven was not to him very different to earth."*

Fred Brown

Fred Brown, D. D.

Evangelist

(1909-   )

The name of Fred Brown in evangelism is something similar to saying "sterling in silver." For forty-two years, ever since his graduation from Bob Jones University in 1933, Evangelist Fred Brown has been a shining, sterling example of an evangelist. His revivals and ministry have a long, lasting effect. He wears a ring of authority, sincerity, reality and eternity in his campaigns. Pastors and churches have him back again and again. He wears well. Yes, sterling is the right word to describe Evangelist Fred Brown.

Brown was born in Birmingham, Alabama, August 23, 1909, and was born again just across the road from his birthplace. That second birth was at the age of seven and in an old-fashioned Presbyterian protracted meeting. That night the preacher pictured Hell so vividly that Brown explains of the experience: "Hell was so real I could smell the fumes from the pit and I could hear the screams of the dying and I could see myself and the worm and the fire that is not quenched."

Until that service Brown had believed he was an innocent seven-year-old boy, but during that sermon he realized that he was a sinner—a sinner lost and on his way to that Hell. When the preacher proclaimed Christ as the One who could save sinners from Hell, Brown left his chair, went forward and confessed his sins to Christ and was converted. And as he has tellingly told, "There never has been a doubt in my mind from that hour to this that I was

42 PROFILES IN EVANGELISM

saved." (It is evident that we ought to get more six, seven and eight-year-olds under such kind of preaching on Sundays and in revival crusades! Amen!)

It was not until he was nineteen years old that Fred Brown felt any definite call to preach, however. Faithful in his church life, satisfied as a department store employee, Brown began to fight that call from Heaven.

But about one month later, at one o'clock in the morning, Fred Brown climbed a hill, kneeled under a tree, and then and there surrendered his life to Christ to preach the Gospel—and especially as an evangelist. Brown has never been anything else.

He has ministered across the nation and across the seas. He has ministered in citywide crusades and in local church campaigns. And despite singular success in cooperative crusades with thousands professing Christ, Fred Brown is basically a local church evangelist and devotes the greatest amount of his time to that kind of ministry. Brown insists, "I would far rather have a good church meeting than a poor citywide meeting. I don't think any individual church gets the same blessing out of a meeting where many churches are cooperating as they do when they have an evangelist in their own church and concentrate upon their own membership, getting them out and personally winning people to Jesus Christ."

Evangelist Brown also is a noted conference speaker—Gull Lake, Maranatha, Mount Hermon, Schroon Lake and very often in his home church, Highland Park Baptist Church, Chattanooga, Tennessee. It is Chattanooga where the Brown's make their home. Mrs. Brown is director of music at the church and a married daughter is professor of speech at Tennessee Temple Schools.

Brown's campaigns are characterized by great Bible teaching and evangelistic preaching. Sinners get saved, and they, along with the other saints, start living for the Lord, working, witnessing and winning the lost. Aye, his converts stick!

In relation to this, Brown relates:

"I used to be afraid that I wouldn't get many decisions when I was a young preacher, but I see so many decisions being made today that never pan out. I'm more afraid of getting a false decision than no decision."

And he adds:

"I think a lot of evangelism is scorched-earth evangelism. I think it is possible to go into a church and try to force folks into decisions that have not been brought about by the working of the Holy Spirit. I think we can make folks make decisions with their heads that never affect their hearts. I am afraid that a lot of these great numbers that are reported today are just such in light of the fact that they never show up in church again after they supposedly made a decision. I am a great believer in allowing the Holy Spirit to do His work. Preach faithfully the Word of God, sow the proper seed, pluck the fruit that is ripe and depend on God to bring the increase of His pleasure. I think we ought to be more concerned with doing something more lasting than something that is temporary and looks good for awhile, but the results are only a handful of smoke."

Again and again in Fred Brown's ministry you detect these major motives. "We have to stand before the Bema seat of Christ one day and give account of our ministries and I certainly want to be able to have at least some reward". . ."I want to see what I do magnify Him and prove to be a blessing to the churches where I minister." . . ."We desire above everything else to be used of the Lord Jesus Christ in bringing folks to Him."

Yes, as suggested earlier, the name of Dr. Fred Brown in evangelism is surely something similar to saying "sterling" in silver.

Pray for this man—and pray for men of his kind when you pray for evangelists—*and pray for them every day!*

E. Howard Cadle

E. Howard Cadle—from profligate to preacher, from unbridled passions to unimpeachable principles, from petty and professional gambler to a prince in prayer, from home breaker to home builder, from errant son of a loving mother to earnest soul winner of his living, loving Master, Jesus Christ; that, in a few words, summarizes one of evangelism's interesting and important sons. Yet, Howard Cadle is relatively unknown to his generation. Not so forty years ago. The name of Howard Cadle, the Cadle Tabernacle, and Cadle's radio broadcast, the "Morning Prayer Period," were household terms across middle America.

Born in Washington County, Indiana, "down where they do not raise much of anything except Democrats and sassafrass," Cadle soon became the black sheep of four children born to a dedicated Christian mother and a drunkard father, who later was converted.

At the age of twelve, Cadle was a wild, wayward youth, drinking liquor and destined to be in the penitentiary before he was twenty. By the grace of God—in answer to a mother's persistent, patient prayers—Cadle avoided that pronounced appointment. At nineteen he married and moved to Oklahoma. But he never moved out of the range of his mother's prayers. *"Always remember, Son, that at eight o'clock every night I'll be kneeling beside your bed, asking God to protect my precious boy,"* she promised.

Marriage slowed Cadle's course into sin for a short season, but soon he was back to his drinking, then into gambling, then adultery, and later into the slot machine rackets, moving back to Indiana where he became "Slot

46   PROFILES IN EVANGELISM

Machine King," his empire embracing Indiana, Illinois and Kentucky.

One night in a drinking, gambling spree Cadle turned to murder. Enraged, he pulled his gun and shot at his intended victim—but the weapon never fired! Someone knocked the revolver from his hand—*it was exactly 8:00 P.M.! A mother's prayers had "kept" her son from the electric chair!*

Soon a state Supreme Court wiped out his rackets' empire—declaring "slots" gambling devices. His syndicate was busted, but his bent to sin was not broken. Reveling with gamblers and harlots was his sole desire; yea, shamefully, his practice even the nights his children were born. But sin's payday eventually comes to everyone who sows its seeds, and Cadle was no exception. One day he awoke to some startling realities: his finances were exhausted, his health dissipated—six months to live. No friends, no money, no health, the profligate but prodigal Cadle went back home. His mother "gathered him in her arms tenderly, covered his swollen face in kisses," and in that hallowed hour he confessed, "Mother, I'm tired of sin. I've broken your heart, betrayed my wife, broken my marriage vows—I'd like to be saved, but I've sinned too much."

His mother kissed him tenderly, replying, "Son, I've prayed twelve years to hear you say what you have just said." She got out her Bible, opened its pages and read Isaiah 1:18: "Come now, and let us reason together, saith the Lord: though your sins be as scarlet, they shall be as white as snow; though they be red like crimson, they shall be as wool."

That morning, March 14, 1914, E. Howard Cadle was saved. He turned to his wife, "Forgive me for all the wrongs I've done to you, Ola." She tearfully kissed her husband, mingling tears of rejoicing with tears of repentance, "I have forgiven you—long ago, Honey."

Cadle had trusted Christ for the saving of his soul, next he trusted Him for the preserving of his life that was threatened with death in six months, a faith God honored with a fruitful and full life.

Early in his conversion Cadle learned the first of lasting lessons that God honors His children who trust and obey Him. He started a *family prayer period!* (Does that sound familiar?) And he started tithing—one dollar and forty cents out of his payday of fourteen dollars a week salary. Cadle soon lost that job for telling the truth. But God ruled and overruled and Cadle caught on at the National Biscuit Company. His first week's tithe was $3.00—a tenth of a $30 paycheck. If the con artist who had lived by his wits during his wicked days was surprised at such goodness of God to his obediences, consider the shock he must have experienced a few years later when, as an owner of a chain of shoe repair businesses, he asked counsel of a friend, no less the governor of Indiana, Governor Goodrich. He challenged Cadle, "Buy them out." Cadle commented, "Can't. Don't have the money." The governor got his bank on the telephone, "Put $40,000 to Howard Cadle's credit and charge my account with it."

Cadle cried out, "Two and one half years before no one would have trusted me with a yellow dog. Now the governor is trusting me with $40,000 with no security except my signature."

Cadle continued increasing his giving to God until his tithe amounted to 75%. But burning in his heart was a burden for revival. He had financed a great Louisville crusade which had lasted for a year. Then his soul was stirred for Indianapolis and a revival with Gipsy Smith. It was in preparation for that campaign that Cadle Tabernacle was conceived, a vast 10,000-seat structure to be named after and dedicated to the memory of his mother whose prayers had saved his soul from Hell.

The construction of the tabernacle stirred up intense opposition by the Methodist Ministerial Association, a struggle that soon became front-page news not only in Indianapolis but in over 500 AP newspapers across the nation. The story of Cadle's conversion, his mother's

48 *PROFILES IN EVANGELISM*

prayers, the construction of the Tabernacle and their pictures became common concern to multitudes.

The Tabernacle was completed. The first day's service sounds something like the chronicle of one of Israel's or the early church's great days: 10,000 in attendance, a choir of 1,485 voices, 200 coming to Christ after Smith's sermon; an offering of $10,400. It was an emotion-charged service. The choir sang, "There Is a Fountain Filled With Blood," Cadle's mother's favorite hymn. Asked to speak, she could only simply say, "Praise the Lord for His everlasting goodness," to which Cadle commented to the crowd, "Mother could not make a speech, but she certainly knows how to pray." And he thrillingly testified of that Tabernacle: "If there be any glory, or any crown to be awarded, I want to give it to my blessed Redeemer, my Christ who saved me; and if there be any crown to spare, I want to place it upon the brow of my sainted mother, whose prayers saved me from a drunkard's grave, and whose faithfulness to the Master's cause on earth has made possible this magnificent Tabernacle to be named in her honor and memory."

Until that time Cadle had done some preaching, but his interests in evangelism had been essentially in the areas of a promoter and financer of campaigns. Crises came in his life. He had always been interested and involved in politics and he won endorsement to the governor of Indiana by his party. About the same time he lost control of the Tabernacle. It was then Cadle surrendered to Christ's call to preach! And it was after that that Cadle rallied support to repossess the Tabernacle and restore it to its original purpose: *evangelism and revival!*

He began the broadcast, "The Nation's Family Prayer Period," called B. R. Lakin to be his associate, and he and the Tabernacle experienced their greatest efforts and effect for evangelism. Each morning the sweet strains of Mrs. Cadle's voice called America to its knees, *"E'er you left your room this morning, did you think to pray. . . ?"*

Only eternity can ever reveal the full results of those

momentous morning broadcasts made live over WLW, Cincinnati, a powerful radio voice that then covered much of the nation. Only eternity can reveal the results of the Tabernacle's great pulpit ministry—Cadle, Lakin, and many other of God's choicest, noblest preachers. Only eternity can reveal the results of the life and labors of Howard Cadle. Untrained academically for the ministry, he nevertheless was a power for God—his testimony was simple, straightforward, strong, speaking to the heart. He exalted the Saviour, honored his mother, magnified prayer, proved the saving, satisfying, sustaining, supplying power of God's salvation purchased with Christ's blood.

Such we see in a sampling of a Cadle sermon:

> And until He calls me, I shall preach the same kind of a Gospel that saved my mother and father; the kind that saved me, your humble servant. It will be the same Gospel that caused my sainted mother to walk across twenty acres of plowed fields on Wednesday nights, when she was worn and weary from her daily toil on that hilly Southern Indiana farm, to pray for me at prayer meeting. I shall preach that kind of Gospel, I repeat, to the sin-cursed world, this bruised and heartless world.

> And when I have gone to the last city and preached my last sermon, and when I have offered my last prayer for the last sinner, when this old body of mine is worn and ready to crumble back to dust, and when my loved ones have gathered around my bed and the death gurgle is heard in my throat, when the old world is receding and Heaven is opening a way, I stand in the presence of Him whom I have preached and loved and have not seen, I want the first 1,000 years to sit at His feet and say, "Thank You, Jesus, for saving me that dark and stormy day from a drunkard's and a gambler's Hell."

William Carey

William Carey

Missionary-Evangelist

(1761-1834)

"Shoemaker by trade, but scholar, linguist and missionary by God's training," William Carey was one of God's giants in the history of evangelism! One of his biographers, F. Dealville Walker, wrote of Carey: "He, with a few contemporaries, was almost singlehanded in conquering the prevailing indifference and hostility to missionary effort; Carey developed a plan for missions, and printed his amazing *Enquiry*; he influenced timid and hesitating men to take steps to the evangelizing of the world." Another wrote of him, "Taking his life as a whole, it is not too much to say that he was the greatest and most versatile Christian missionary sent out in modern times."

Carey was born in a small thatched cottage in Paulerspury, a typical Northamptonshire village in England, August 17, 1761, of a weaver's family. When about eighteen he left the Church of England to "follow Christ" and to ". . .go forth unto him without the camp, bearing his reproach." At first he joined the Congregational church at Hackleton where he was an apprentice shoemaker. It was there he married in 1791. And it was at Hackleton he began making five-mile walks to Olney in his quest for more spiritual truth. Olney was a stronghold of the Particular Baptists, the group that Carey cast his lot with after his baptism, October 5, 1783. Two years later he moved to Moulton to become a schoolmaster—and a year later he became pastor of the small Baptist congregation there.

PROFILES IN EVANGELISM

It was in Moulton that Carey heard the missionary call. In his own words he cried, "My attention to missions was first awakened after I was at Moulton, by reading the *Last Voyage of Captain Cook*." To many, Cook's *Journal* was a thrilling story of adventure, but to Carey it was a revelation of human need! He then began to read every book that had any bearing on the subject. (This, along with his language study—for at twenty-one years of age Carey had mastered Latin, Greek, Hebrew and Italian, and was turning to Dutch and French. One well called his shoemaker's cottage "Carey's College," for as he cobbled shoes along with his preaching he never sat at his bench without some kind of a book before him.)

The more he read and studied, the more convinced he was "the peoples of the world need Christ." He read, he made notes, he made a great leather globe of the world and, one day, in the quietness of his cobbler's shop—not in some enthusiastic missionary conference—Carey heard the call: "If it be the duty of all men to believe the Gospel. . .then it be the duty of those who are entrusted with the Gospel to endeavor to make it known among all nations." And Carey sobbed out, *"Here am I; send me!"*

To surrender was one thing—to get to the field was quite another problem. There were no missionary societies and there was no real missionary interest. When Carey propounded this subject for discussion at a ministers meeting, "Whether the command given to the apostles to teach all nations was not obligatory on all succeeding ministers to the end of the world, seeing that the accompanying promise was of equal extent," Dr. Ryland shouted, "Young man, sit down: when God pleases to convert the heathen, He will do it without your aid or mine." Andrew Fuller added his feelings as resembling the unbelieving captain of Israel, who said, "If the Lord should make windows in heaven, might such a thing be!"

But Carey persisted. He later said of his ministry, *"I can plod!"* And he was a man who "always resolutely determined never to give up on any point or particle of

William Carey

anything on which his mind was set until he had arrived at a clear knowledge of his subject."

Thus Carey wrote his famed *Enquiry Into the Obligations of the Christians to Use Means for the Conversion of the Heathen.* In this masterpiece on missions Carey answered arguments, surveyed the history of missions from apostolic times, surveyed the entire known world as to countries, size, population and religions, and dealt with the practical application of how to reach the world for Christ!

And he prayed. And he pled. And he plodded. And he persisted. And he preached—especially his epoch-producing message, "EXPECT GREAT THINGS FROM GOD. ATTEMPT GREAT THINGS FOR GOD." The result of that message preached at Nottingham, May 30, 1792—and all the other missionary ministries of Carey—produced the Particular Baptist Missionary Society, formed that Fall at Kettering on October 2, 1792. A subscription was started and, ironically, Carey could not contribute any money toward it except the pledge of the profit from his book, *The Enquiry.*

It was in 1793 that Carey went to India. At first his wife was reluctant to go—so Carey set off to go nevertheless, but after two returns from the docks to persuade her again, Dorothy and his children accompanied him. They arrived with a Dr. Thomas at the mouth of the Hooghly in India in November, 1793. There were years of discouragement (no Indian convert for seven years), debt, disease, deterioration of his wife's mind, death, but by the grace of God—and by the power of the Word—Carey continued and conquered for Christ!

When he died at 73 (1834), he had seen the Scriptures translated and printed into forty languages, he had been a college professor, and had founded a college at Serampore. He had seen India open its doors to missionaries, he had seen the edict passed prohibiting *sati* (burning widows on the funeral pyres of their dead husbands) and he had seen converts for Christ.

On his deathbed Carey called out to a missionary friend, *"Dr. Duff! You have been speaking about Dr. Carey; when I am gone, say nothing about Dr. Carey—speak about Dr. Carey's God."* That charge was symbolic of Carey, considered by many to be a "unique figure, towering above both contemporaries and successors" in the ministry of missions.

John Carrara

Evangelist

(1913-   )

The first evangelist I ever heard was John Carrara. I was a teenager, recently saved, and very ignorant of the Word of God and the work of God. The announcement that "evangelistic meetings with John Carrara will begin next Sunday" sounded very interesting to me because I was ignorant of what such meetings would be. I soon would learn.

The next Sunday, a young, slim, handsome Italian man was introduced to the congregation. In staccato sentences the evangelist began an earnest entreaty for sinners to get saved and get right with God. As he continued his message, he challenged the Christians to seek the lost, to live clean lives for Christ, to pray, to read their Bibles, to stand up and be counted. He told of his conversion from Catholicism to Christ and what it cost him to take his stand, but what peace and the presence of God his pardoned soul had experienced since his conversion. Nobody needed to persuade me to be back that Sunday night. I purposed then and there I would hear every message of that man. That was nearly thirty-six years ago, but I am sure my memory misses not when I say I made every meeting.

It was my first taste of evangelism and suffice it to say, I was converted to that kind of Bible-based, sinner-seeking and saving, Christian-reviving, church-building, Christ-exalting evangelism that results from earnest, fervent, honest, forthright evangelistic preaching of the Word of God! As I pen these pages, I thank God again that my first

John Carrara

impressionable years as a teenager were when I sat under the ministry of the man sent from God—John Carrara!

Carrara was converted to Christ from Catholicism as a teenager in Fairview, New Jersey, although he was born in Nyack, New York, four days after Christmas in 1913. John had been dedicated by his parents to be a priest and was thoroughly indoctrinated in the doctrines and dogmas of the Roman church and as a teenager he was devoted to living with a rigid conformity to the moral and religious demands of that church.

However, God shattered John's false security in his religious rites, spoke to the hollow hopelessness of his soul, and saved him. The weapons were a close companion (a Protestant) at school—*and the Word of God!* The classmate, "a born-again believer," reasoned with John from the Scriptures of his need of Christ and soon Carrara *"realized his religion was a mere outward ritual while his friend seemed to posseess an inward reality."* More and more he desired the same certainty and reality, even to where he was willing to visit the "Protestant" church. In those days there was no so-called ecumenical spirit that permitted Catholics that *privilege!*

On that initial visit John saw an inscription of John 3:16 printed above the baptistry. Nothing the preacher said seemingly impressed him—but that Scripture struck his spirit as a bolt out of the blue: *". . .shall never perish!" ". . .shall never perish!" ". . .shall never perish!"* That was it! That was what he wanted! Something was born in his heart that hour—God's Spirit was speaking to his soul!

Under deep conviction of his sin and his personal need of the Saviour, and realizing his own religion offered him no hope, no Heaven, no help from God, John purposed to return to the next meeting that he might get another glimpse of those wonderful words printed on the church wall.

And he did! And that Wednesday night during the invitation at the prayer meeting, John Carrara, standing in the pew, called upon Christ to be his own personal Saviour!

In his own words, what followed is like reading fiction. News spread through the town like wildfire. Upon arrival home his father beat him until a shoulder was dislocated. His brothers and sisters taunted and profaned him—"Protestant." He was taken out of school. He was disowned and finally driven from home. For three years he lived as best he could, hungry most of the time, finally becoming known as a "walking skeleton." During this time Carrara contracted tuberculosis, but, miraculously, X-rays later revealed he had been healed by the Lord of that dread, death-dealing disease.

Shortly after his conversion the Lord led the then sixteen-year-old youth into evangelism, a ministry that he has faithfully and continually labored in since. First, it was open doors in churches in metropolitan New York, then, in increasingly widening arcs until now he has ministered in forty-four states and from Ottawa to Vancouver, British Columbia. Dr. Carrara comments that he has preached in every place imaginable: churches, schoolhouses, opera houses, theaters, halls, tents, auditoriums, armories, basements, barns, mansions, missions, conferences, camp grounds, street corners, brush arbors, colleges, Bible schools, seminaries, prisons, reformatories, hotels—aye, anywhere and everywhere from "A" to "Z," Carrara has probably preached Christ there!

And that is his ministry: preaching Christ and the Book! He uses no tricks, no magic, no gimmicks to get a crowd, hold a crowd or convert a crowd. Carrara preaches the Bible! And Carrara's successes have stemmed from his unswerving loyalties to that Bible. He knows what the Word did for him, and he knows what it will do for others. That pastors and people appreciate that kind of evangelism is evidenced by the fact Carrara has been called to return to some churches as many as seven times for campaigns. That sinners are reached and redeemed by his brand of evangelism is evidenced by the hundreds of converts across North America. Among them—his parents and several brothers and sisters! Amen!

Recently Evangelist Carrara and his wife (a convert in a Meadville, Pennsylvania, campaign and a constant companion with him in his ministry, now) had a meal in my home with my family and some converted Catholic neighbors. And after the meal I had an opportunity to hear John Carrara preach again.

It was thirty-six years ago I heard him preach the first time. He is no longer that bony, skinny youth. But I saw the same blazing eyes, the same passionate preacher, the same expenditure of energy, the same authoritative message, the same pleading for souls and the same exalting Christ! Amen! For, as a news commentator wrote of John Carrara in a secular report recently, "Consider it coincidental or providential that his name should be taken from the famous Carrara marble (meaning white) which is called rock eternal, even he is the exponent of Him who is the Rock of Ages, and the foundation of the church of the living God."

Peter Cartwright

Peter Cartwright
Backwoods Evangelist
(1785-1872)

The men who evangelized early 19th century America had to be men at their best. They had to be men with hearts hot for the lost, men with souls sweet with their Lord, men with spirits unshakable in the light of the laxness and lukewarmness of Christian living and the looseness and licentious living of the lost in those frontier days. Need it be added that those men had to possess bodies that could brave and best the maximum in physical punishment and privations during wilderness travels.

Put down the name of Peter Cartwright, Methodist circuit rider, when you count up those illustrious worthies of itinerant evangelism in early America!

That it took a real call from God to be a backwoods, circuit-riding preacher can be evinced from these excerpts from Cartwright's autobiography penned in 1856:

> People, unaquainted with frontier life, and especially frontier life fifty or sixty years ago, can form but a very imperfect idea of the sufferings and hardships underwent at that day, when Methodist preachers went from fort to fort, from camp to camp, from cabin to cabin, with or without road, or path. We walked on dirt floors for carpets, sat on stools or benches for chairs, ate on puncheon tables (large casks), had forked sticks and pocket or butcher knives and forks, slept on bear, deer or buffalo skins before a fire, or sometimes on the ground in the open air, had our saddles or saddlebags for pillows, and one new suit of clothes of homespun was ample clothing for one year for an early preacher in the West. We crossed creeks and large rivers without bridges or ferry

PROFILES IN EVANGELISM

> boats, often swam them on horseback, or crossed on trees that had fallen over the streams, often waded waist deep; and if by chance we got a dugout, or a canoe, to cross in ourselves, and swim our horses by, it was quite a treat.

Cartwright had that call. And he had the courage that went with that call. Circuit riders had to be ready to defend their lives, their library (his was a Bible, a hymnbook and a book of discipline), their little store of possessions that could be carried on their saddle and—always—their testimony for Christ. Sometimes it took a pistol, sometimes physical force, sometimes preaching—always it took prayer! Many are the accounts in his journal when Cartwright cleaned up on some bullies so he could continue preaching the claims of Christ.

No reference to his courage would be complete without this story of Saturday night in the Cumberland mountains. Unable to reach a Christian home, he had to spend Saturday night and the Lord's Day in a hotel where a drinking, dancing party was being held. He had asked for permission to preach but had been refused. Later, a "beautiful, ruddy young lady," learning he was a preacher, asked him for a dance. Sensing an opportunity to preach, Cartwright accompanied her to the floor. Suddenly he exclaimed that he never undertook any matter of importance without first asking the blessing of God upon it, and grasping her hand he cried out, "Let us all kneel on the floor and pray." And he did with "all his power of soul." The girl tried to break his grasp, the fiddler fled to the kitchen, some wept aloud, crying out for mercy. Then Cartwright arose, preached, led in some hymns, and the meeting continued nearly all night. The young lady was converted, a society was organized, and a revival broke out in those mountains.

Another time Cartwright was invited to preach in a large downtown Presbyterian church in Nashville. Announcing his text, "What shall it profit a man if he shall gain the whole world and lose his own soul," he was interrupted by the pastor's whispering, *"General Jackson has come in. General Jackson has come in."* Indignant at the interruption because of a celebrity entering the church, Cartwright called out: "Who is General Jackson? If he doesn't get his soul converted, God will damn him as quick as a Guinea Negro." The General approved of Cartwright's courage and confided to him, "If I had a few thousand such independent, fearless officers as you are, and a well-drilled army, I could take old England."

Cartwright was also compassionate. In one account it is related that one day he was catechizing some young Methodist children. He gave out the question, "And who is the Good Shepherd?" Immediately, and in one voice, the children cried out, "Peter Cartwright!" Need anything else be added?

Cartwright was born in Amherst County, near the James River, Virginia, September 1, 1785, of poor parents who moved to Kentucky, where, as a youth, he lived a wasted, wicked life until he was converted from his cards, dancing, fast horses and wanton ways at the age of sixteen after a sacramental meeting. Cartwright joined the Methodists and was one of their leading lights that led them from a hated handful to a multi-membered host. He became a presiding elder at eighteen and traveled for fifty-three years in eleven circuits, twelve districts in Kentucky, Tennessee, and Illinois, preaching over 14,000 sermons and receiving into the church 10,000 members.

Suffice it to say, Cartwright was a different disciple in Methodism than many of its present preachers. He preached on the fact of sin; the lostness of sinners; the living, loving Lord Jesus who saves; the shed blood that delivers from sin; a Heaven to win and a hot Hell to shun; repentance, restitution, etc., in contrast to the ecumenical evangelism and social action of Methodism, for the most part, today.

Would to God there might be many men today with Cartwright's kind of call, courage, and compassion, who would stand and be counted as men who will sell out to calling our nation back to God for revival and righteousness!

J. Wilbur Chapman

J. Wilbur Chapman

Evangelist

(1859-1918)

Put it down: J. W. Chapman was another product of the "personal touch"—the personal touch of his Sunday school teacher! In this respect, Chapman was another in that long line of soul-winning worthies who traced their coming to Christ through the personal influences of a friend: Wesley, Spurgeon, Moody, among others of whom I have written in these profiles!

Chapman's confession of Christ came about one Sunday afternoon when a visiting speaker addressed his school. *Chapman attended two schools each Sunday in his Richmond, Indiana, birthplace—the Presbyterian in the morning and his deceased mother's church, Grace Methodist Episcopal, in the afternoon.* At the close of his address the speaker made an appeal to the scholars to stand and confess Christ. Chapman wrote of that experience thusly:

> I think every boy in my class rose to his feet with the exception of myself. I found myself reasoning thus: Why should I rise, my mother was a saint; my father is one of the truest men I know; my home teaching has been all that a boy could have; I know about Christ and I think I realize His power to save. While I was thus reasoning, my Sunday school teacher (Mrs. C. C. Binkley, wife of Senator Binkley), with tears in her eyes, leaned around back of the other boys and looking straight at me, as I turned toward her, said, "Would it not be best for you to rise?" And when she saw I still hesitated, she put her hand under my elbow and lifted me up just a little bit, and I stood upon my feet. I can never describe my

PROFILES IN EVANGELISM

> emotions. I do not know that that was the time of my conversion but I do know it was the day when one of the most profound impressions of my life was made. Through all these years I have never forgotten it, and it was my teacher who influenced me thus to take the stand—it was her personal touch that gave me courage to rise before the church and confess my Saviour.

A few years later, as a student at Lake Forest University, near Chicago, in a D. L. Moody campaign, Chapman received absolute assurance of his salvation and "his acceptance with God" when dealt with personally by Mr. Moody, himself! And later it was Moody, again, who personally encouraged Chapman, then a pastor, to enter wholly into evangelistic work.

Chapman held four pastorates but devoted more than half of his ministry to evangelism that carried him to major American cities, Canada, the British Isles, Japan, China, Australia, and many other countries. He was also the first director of the Winona Lake Bible Conference and contributed much to two other summer conferences—one at Montreat, North Carolina, and one at Stony Brook, Long Island. Chapman was a Presbyterian, and in 1903 was made Executive Secretary of the Presbyterian General Assembly's committee on evangelism. He was also elected as moderator of the General Assembly in 1918, the year in which he died at the age of 59.

Chapman was the author of several books of evangelistic sermons and books about evangelism: *And Judas Iscariot, And Peter, Another Mile, S. H. Hadley of Water Street, Revival Sermons, The Lost Crown, The Personal Touch, Present-Day Evangelism, Problems of the Work.* Preached and printed in the early years of this Twentieth Century, these pages will be profitable for evangelists, pastors and their people to read and heed today! Chapman's messages were marked by a simplicity, a warmth, an appeal to the Scriptures. They spoke to the heart and challenged the soul.

Elgin Moyer wrote of Chapman's ministry:

> A cultured, earnest, enthusiastic, and sane evangelist,

never coarse, vulgar, or thoughtless in preaching or in his manner of life. In preaching, calm but forceful, emotional but not dramatic. In setting up, campaigns planned well, a well-balanced man.

Chapman evaluated his own ministry thusly: *"I commit myself, however, only to that evangelism which strengthens the church, cheers the minister, and makes plain the way to the cross for the sinner."*

Analyzed in any avenue, Chapman was a product of, a preacher of, and a practicer of personal work, or, the "personal touch," as he was prone to call it. As he often said it:

All along the way I have been brought in contact with men whom God has signally blessed, and I am persuaded that there are many today whose hearts are hungering for a blessing, who are waiting as I was myself, for someone to speak to them personally, and help them out of darkness into light, out of a certain kind of bondage into glorious freedom. The personal touch in Christian work, to me, means everything.

Aye, and it is just as true in the 1970's.

Jonathan Edwards

Jonathan Edwards

Revivalist

(1703-1758)

A few years ago I stood on the spot where, doubtlessly, the most famous sermon ever preached in America was delivered. The place was Enfield, Connecticut. The date the sermon was delivered, July 8, 1741. The subject of the sermon was *"Sinners in the Hands of an Angry God."* The preacher was Jonathan Edwards. The results were phenomenal. As Edwards preached (actually, he *read* the manuscript to the congregation), strong men and women cried out for mercy, pleading with the preacher, "Is there no way of escape?" as Edwards exhorted them in such sentences as these:

> His wrath towards you burns like fire. He looks upon you as worthy of nothing else but to be cast into the fire. He is of purer eyes than to bear to have you in His sight. You are ten thousand times more abominable in His eyes than the most hateful venomous serpent is in ours. You have offended Him infinitely more than ever a stubborn rebel did his prince; and yet, it is nothing but His hand that holds you from falling into the fire every moment. . . .O sinner, consider the fearful danger you are in! It is a great furnace of wrath, a wide and bottomless pit, full of the fire of wrath, that you are held over in the hand of that God whose wrath is provoked and incensed as much against you as against any of the damned in Hell. You hang by a slender thread, with the flames of divine wrath flashing about it and ready any minute to singe it and burn it asunder; and you have no interest in any Mediator and nothing to lay hold of to save yourself, nothing to keep off the flames of wrath, nothing of your own, nothing that you have done,

PROFILES IN EVANGELISM

nothing that you can do, to induce God to spare you one moment.

Hundreds were converted when they heard that sermon—a subpoena from the skies. And it was that kind of preaching that produced the "Great Awakening," the revival of the 18th century that under God, spared the American colonies the horrible holocaust and blood bath that France suffered during the French Revolution. Doubtlessly, Jonathan Edwards was the chiefest American who championed the cause of revival and called the colonists back to God and the Bible, although his efforts were confined mostly to the Connecticut valley.

As pastor of the church in Northampton, Massachusetts, Edwards saw revival break out in his staid membership in 1734. Doubtlessly the sermon that helped bring it to pass was, "That Every Mouth May Be Stopped." The directness, the passionate earnestness, the searching indictment of Edward's ministry is manifest in these charges leveled at his congregation:

> Look over your past life. . . .How little regard you have had for the Scriptures, to the Word preached, to the Sabbaths and sacraments! What low thoughts you have had of God and what high thoughts of yourselves! Many of you by the bad examples you have set, by corrupting the minds of others, by your sinful conversation, by leading them in sin and by the mischief you have done in human society other ways, have been guilty of these things that have tended to other's damnation. If God should forever cast you off and destroy you, it would be agreeable to your treatment of Himself, of Christ, of your neighbors and yourself.

The congregation did not go forward after the message. But they called upon the pastor for counsel in their condemned state—*and were converted!* Edwards estimated that "300 of the 670 communicants were savingly brought home to Christ." The revival lasted six months. He later wrote of those experiences:

> The town seemed to be full of the presence of God. The noise amongst the dry bones waxed louder and louder. The revival struck the hearts first of the young people and

Jonathan Edwards

then of their elders all over the town. . . .The tavern was soon empty. People had done with their quarrels, backbiting and intermeddling with other men's matters.

In 1740, another wave of revival broke out that dwarfed the earlier revival at Northampton. It was the "Great Awakening" indeed. Edwards, again and again, left his pulpit to preach in neighboring towns where revival fires were lighted.

However, it was in Northampton, the scene of so many successes, that Edwards received his most crushing defeat. In 1750, his church dismissed him as pastor because of his insistence upon a regenerated membership and the abolishment of the "half-way covenant" membership common to the churches in the colonies. Denied pulpits in which to preach, Edwards became a missionary to the Indians at Stockbridge. Here he devoted himself to his writings as well as preaching. And, in February, 1758, he was installed as president of Princeton University. This was to be the briefest of ministries because on March 22, a month later, Edwards was dead, a victim of smallpox, a scourge to which his wife, Sarah, was also to succumb six months later.

Edwards was a powerful, intellectual giant in New England. Born October 5, 1703 (the same year John Wesley was born), in East Windsor, Connecticut, he was studying Latin at six years of age, and read Latin, Greek and Hebrew when he went to college at 13. He graduated from Yale at 17. He was a Calvinist, "though his inquisitive and speculative mind ranged far beyond the boundaries of inherited theology. . . ."

"Though Edwards was cut off in the fulness of his power, his life does not suggest incompleteness," one biographer wrote. *"Rather, it rounded into a perfect whole because it had a fixed and single center—that burning core of conviction that had flashed upon him in his youth. . . .God as a Being who was to him at once majestic and holy, beautiful and loving, and in comparison with whom everything else in the world of nature and of*

man was as nothing. That is why he thought of people and dealt with them in terms of their rebellion, their self-deception, and their aspiration for the life abundant, their inner conflicts, and their specious contentment with less than their best."

Doubtlessly, this conviction was one of the most real reasons why Jonathan Edwards made such a consummate contribution for revival in the colonies when the "temperature of religion was only a moderate warmth and the passion and purpose of the first generation colonists had been spent!"

Who can doubt or deny but what America today needs some men of similar stripe and spirit!

Christmas Evans

Evangelist

(1766-1838)

He was described as the "gargantuan preacher: the tallest, stoutest, greatest man ever known." And another added: "He appeared as an Anak whose head is covered with thick, coarse, black hair. His gait unwieldly, his limbs unequal. He has but one eye—if it might be called an eye—more properly, a brilliant star over against a ghastly empty socket." You believe it, as an evangelist, Evans has had few equals when you measure men by their spiritual power with God and men, or by their spellbinding pulpit delivery.

His uncommon first name resulted from the date of his birth—December 25, 1766—for he was the "Christmas bach" (Christmas lad) of a poor shoemaker, Samuel, and his wife, Joanna, of Cardiganshire, Wales. In the poverty and obscurity of his birth, the infant Evans was somewhat akin to the Saviour he would so powerfully preach one day. Though his parents were poor in the finances of the world, they were rich in faith and love for the Lord, and the young Christmas commenced childhood with all the advantages of such a Christian atmosphere.

However, when he was only nine years old, Christmas's dad died, and his mother finally, with real reluctance, had to farm out her children to her family and friends. Christmas's lot was to live with an uncle, a cruel, infidel farmer. The young Evans soon began to follow in his uncle's wicked ways and by the time Christmas was seventeen he was an uneducated (not even able to read),

Christmas Evans

unsaved, untamed youth running and living like a savage beast with a group of wild mountain young men.

But the grace of God that is greater than all our sins showed itself strong to the saving of Evan's sinful soul. Somehow he kept alive despite his wild, wicked ways of heedlessness and carelessness which brought him to the doors of death many times. And somehow Evans got under some gospel preaching—preached in power and probing plainness by the Rev. David Davies. Evan's sins became abhorrent to him, new and holy desires were awakened in his soul, unbelievably to the place where Evans wished to preach the Gospel himself. In fact, he and some other similarly sin-smitten youths banded together in a barn to study the Scriptures. It was here that Evans purposed to learn to read and also to memorize the Bible. So ardent was his desire and so able his mentality that he soon memorized preachers' messages and prayers and began to preach them. And as Dr. R. E. Day declared, "He became an overnight sensation!"

But it is doubtful that Evans was truly converted to Christ until three or four years later. Then, in a place of constant doubts and fears, as well as assailed by his dumbness to learn and burdened by the guilt of his sins, Evans was converted to Christ and that crushing burden rolled away and he "received the garment of praise for the spirit of heaviness." And, when he was converted, he was also called, *really called by God,* to preach the Gospel. But that was not all—he was also clobbered by some of his ungodly companions because of his stand for the Saviour. It was at this brutal beating that one blow burst his eye, and for the rest of his life Christmas Evans wore that "ghastly empty socket," becoming known as the "one-eyed preacher of Anglesey."

At twenty-four years of age, he was ordained a Baptist preacher at Lleyn, Caernarvonshire, and became pastor of the church. During that pastorate, Evans often evangelized the coasts of Wales. At the age of forty, he and his wife went to Anglesey. There he lost the fire from his ministry

PROFILES IN EVANGELISM

and his fervor for souls. His ministry became centered in controversy with a group called the Sandemanianists and "his health failed, his joy was departed, a deep nostalgia arose from the olden days he knew in his ministry at Lleyn."

Like a Jacob returning to Bethel, like a David repenting as recorded in Psalm 51, Christmas Evans sought a place to make peace with his God. It was along a lonely mountain road. His record of that repentance and revival reads: "After I had commenced praying, I soon felt as if mountains of snow and ice were melting within me. . . .My tears flowed copiously and I was constrained to cry aloud and pray for the gracious visits of God for the joy of His salvation. I felt my whole spirit relieved of some great bondage, and as if it were rising up from the grave of some severe winter."

He later said his *"soul was set on fire with divine unction and power such as he had never known."* Suffice it to say, he was never the same again. *"Powerful sermons, the breath of Heaven, the weeping, the praising, the returning of sinners to God"* became the standard wherever Evans evangelized. Villages would awaken, their inhabitants pour along the hills and down by the valleys awaiting the coming of Christmas Evans. Revival fires were lighted and fires spread all across the island of Anglesey.

Evans preached for nearly thirty more years, riding his horse, oftentimes his wife riding with him. A July night in 1838, Evans preached his last message at Swansea. Two hours later he descended the pulpit stairs, desperately ill, and declared, "This is my last sermon." It was—and as friends wept for him at his bedside, Evans would interject, "Don't weep for me. Forty and eight years have I ministered in the sanctuary. But I have never ministered without blood in the basin."

And save for a short time it may be articulately added—*and not without revival fire in his soul!!* Amen!

Charles Grandison Finney

Apostolic Evangelism

(1792-1875)

When you read the messages and the ministry of Charles Finney, you get the strange sensation that you are reading pages out of the book of the Acts of the Apostles. Rightly so! For doubtlessly no American evangelist, in his ministry, ever more paralleled the apostolic preaching, passion and power of a Simon Peter or an Apostle Paul as did Charles G. Finney.

Finney, an aspiring young lawyer, was converted to Christ in Adams, New York, on October 10, 1821. Immediately after his conversion he set out to witness for Christ and to realize results few Christians have ever experienced.

One of Finney's biographers wrote:

> Finney went up and down the village street, like a merchant, like a salesman searching for customers, conversing with any with whom he might meet. The "slain of the Lord" fell as if machine-gunned on the village streets. Pious frauds, young Unitarian smart-alecs, booze-makers, the unsaved, scoffers—it made no difference who they were. "A few words spoken to an individual would stick in his heart like an arrow."

As Finney himself spoke of that first day's evangelism, "I believe the Spirit of God made lasting impression upon every one of them. I cannot remember one whom I spoke with who was not converted."

From *personal evangelism* of this kind, it was inevitable that Finney would progress to *preaching evangelism*. Although men were reluctant to ordain him to preach, the

Charles Grandison Finney

Lord had laid His hand on this soul-hungry convert of Christ. "Thus began one of the most remarkable careers in the history of modern evangelism," for, again, Finney's record reads like the book of Acts. He preached out-of-doors, in barns, in schoolhouses, anywhere, everywhere. And anywhere and everywhere he went they realized revival; "revival," as one well wrote, "that began as the gentle breathing of God's Spirit upon the dry bones of dead orthodoxy or a defiant godlessness and became a whirlwind in the ministry of Finney."

Evans Mills, New York, scene of Finney's first campaign, illustrates the truth of that testimony: "The whole town buzzed with profanity against him. They talked of tarring and feathering him, riding him on a rail." But under Finney's typical fearless preaching—preaching that was Spirit-of-God anointed, unsparing against sin, and preaching that demanded a definite, immediate decision—sinners became so smitten with such conviction of sin and awful distress of mind that at all hours of the night "they rushed out to the country where he was staying" to get right with God. Finney later related of this campaign, "When I left the citizens of Evans Mills were in an avalanche of revival power."

Limited space prohibits more than mere mention of his increasing, intense, incendiary evangelism that caused "American cities to flare up like fire points. Gouverneur! Rome! Utica! Auburn! Troy! Wilmington! Philadelphia!" Then it was New York City! Then Rochester! Then Boston! Then America! Then Great Britain!

That Rochester revival must be reviewed. Dr. Beecher related of it:

> That was the greatest work of God, and the greatest revival of religion, that the world has ever seen in so short a time. One hundred thousand were reported as having concerned themselves with churches as a result of this great revival.

Another wrote:

> The whole community was stirred. Religion was the topic of conversation, in the house, in the shop, in the

PROFILES IN EVANGELISM

office, and on the street. . . .The only theater in the city was converted into a livery stable. . . .It is worthy of special notice that a large number of the leading men of the place were among the converts—the lawyers, the judges, the physicians, merchants, bankers. . . .Tall oaks bowed as by the blast of a hurricane. . . .The courts had little to do, and the jail was nearly empty for years afterward.

Beloved, that was Nineteenth Century kind of evangelism. Do we even dare compare it with our Twentieth Century brand of "Smile, smile, give your face a treat" . . ."heavenly sunshine". . ."shake hands with three people around you," self-satisfied, dry-eyed, coldhearted, "easy-come, easy-go" evangelism? *To ask the question is to answer it!* Somehow, may the Spirit of God smite us in our sinfulness and sham. Somehow, may He show us the one, the single, the *supreme need* of our Twentieth Century cities and society which are steeped in sin and strife is for another such spiritual awakening as Charles Finney and his contemporaries experienced under God in the late 1800's.

Would to God that I could put on this page the heart of the revival messages, the revival methods, and the heartbeat of the revival-mastered man—C. G. Finney. It would take a book to do it. However, there is a book: *Finney's Lectures on Revival.* Buy it. Read it. Weep over it. Let it melt and move your heart! Experience its power! Practice its pages!

But in my last paragraph may I make mention of a hunger in my heart. May I plead with every reader of these pages that, beginning today, we commence crying out to the God of Finney, the God of Elijah, the God of the apostles, yea, the God of revival, that He rain upon this sin-soaked, sin-scarred nation a revival; a revival that will result in repentance from sin, righteousness restored, and God's people rejoicing (Ps. 85:6). And in the same breath, may I beg you, again: will you pray daily, dedicatedly, doggedly, yea, desperately that the same living, loving Lord will raise up in our ranks an army of evangelists anointed with the same apostolic authority, enabled with the same Holy Spirit enduement that filled and fired Charles Grandison Finney to be the great force and flame for revival he was for his desperate day!

Mordecai Ham

Evangelist

(1878-1959)

Meet Mordecai F. Ham—another of those old-time evangelists, that worthy handful of men who at the conclusion of the Nineteenth Century and the commencement of the Twentieth Century shook their generation for God, wrought revivals and restored some semblance of righteousness to America such as has never been accomplished since.

Mordecai Ham had a heritage that surely helped spark and shape his message and ministry. "God raised up Ham from three centuries of spiritually-minded men," noteworthy among them, Roger Williams, "pioneer fighter for religious liberty in America."

It was his father's life and his grandfather's death that God used to mold the unforgettable and unalterable aspirations and influences of young Mordecai's spiritual life. Ham "attributed his conversion and spiritual inclinations to the devotional habits of his boyhood home," relating, "We had a family 'revival' every evening. Father (a preacher himself—pastoring as many as six Kentucky country churches at one time) would give us a Bible reading and a sermon; then ask his children to confess any ill conduct of which they had been guilty that day."

When his grandfather (Mordecai F., Sr.) died, the young Mordecai knew he was to preach. As a seven-year-old he had such inclinations—preaching to neighborhood cats and dogs. Once he tried to "Immerse an old tomcat in a rain trough, and when the subject vented all its feline ferocity in objecting to the 'baptism,' little Mordecai threw him down with the disgusted explanation, *'Go on, get sprinkled and go to Hell.' "*

However, Ham had suppressed that call until his grandfather's death. Called back to Bowling Green, Kentucky, to the deathbed of his beloved kin, Mordecai saw the old man breathe his last at four o'clock that February 28, 1899, morning, "point upwards, as though beholding the Lord beckoning him to come home." That moment the 22-year-old Mordecai knew his grandfather's mantle had fallen upon him. He later declared, "Seeing him die did more than anything else to convince me of the reality of Christian experience."

And Ham mirrored much of the old man whose plain preaching influenced Mordecai to be, as he called himself, "A hog-jowl and turnip green" preacher.

However Ham did not quit the road as a traveling salesman and prepare to preach until he married Miss Bessie Simmons of Bowling Green. His preparation was eight months long. During that period of "careful study and prayerful reading the Bible," Ham was appalled to see "the terrible shortcomings of Christendom and how far my own Brethren (Baptists) had wandered from the *New Testament* pattern."

In September, 1901, Ham preached his first sermon. Attending a district association meeting at Bethlehem, Kentucky, with his father, he was shocked to hear the announcement, "The next message will be given by Rev. Mordecai F. Ham, Jr." Unprepared for that unexpected assignment, Mordecai nevertheless mounted the pulpit and preached from Matthew 11:12. That day he was not preaching to cats and dogs, but pastors and messengers from the association; and preaching not on some street or alley, but from the pulpit where his grandfather had preached for forty years! God's blessing was upon him—the congregation was stirred, invitations to preach in other churches were extended and that day Mordecai F. Ham, Jr., entered the ministry.

84   *PROFILES IN EVANGELISM*

In his early days, Ham began a practice he pursued most of his ministry, "He hunted the lowest sinners in the community and, finding them, would pray and plead with them until they were surrendered to Christ."

Ham was fearless in his ministry, strongly denouncing sin in his preaching, carrying the battle to moonshiners, the liquor crowd, confronting rioters, disturbers, opposing modernists, praying down and pronouncing judgment upon those who contested his campaigns.

One instance illustrates his courage and convictions:

> On that second night it seemed all "hell" broke loose as the moonshine crowd stole up around the church and threw rocks at us. They unharnessed the horses, cut the saddle straps and stole everything they could carry off.

Ham went out and confronted the ringleader, who proceeded to pull a knife on him. *"Put up that knife, you coward. If you were not a coward you would not pull a knife on an unarmed man. Now I'm going to ask the Lord either to convert you or to kill you."*

"Do as you _____ please," he snarled at Ham and stalked off. Ham prayed and the bully was dead the next morning. Three others of the gang were killed when a sawmill blew up. That night Ham demanded all the stolen property returned or the Lord might kill someone else. Twenty-four hours later all had been returned but a saddle. Ham announced he was going to lead in prayer, and the one fellow "jumped up and hollered, 'You needn't pray! It will be here in a few minutes,' and it was."

Ham's ministry was mostly citywide and in the Southern states, although he preached in Colorado, Kansas, Ohio, Indiana and Minnesota. Everywhere he left a wake of converts (Billy Graham probably being the most celebrated conversion)—over 300,000 additions in forty years of campaigns, revived churches, community conditions changed.

Just a few examples suffice: In Macon, Georgia, thirteen "houses" of the red-light district were closed—the girls converted. The Ham-Ramsey (his associate and song leader) team, in almost every county in which they held a campaign, saw those counties vote dry in elections where booze was on the ballot. After a meeting in Marlow, Oklahoma, the cashier of the bank reported 75% of uncollected accounts paid! Raleigh, North Carolina, February to April, 5,000 decisions for Christ. Burlington, North Carolina's mayor's letter to local paper: ". . .I must say I have never seen the city of Burlington so thoroughly stirred as it has been by this [Ham] campaign. Every department of our municipal government has felt the wonderful effects of this meeting. . ." *(Burlington Daily Times,* May 20, 1925).

In 1927, Ham retired from evangelism for a brief two years to pastor First Baptist Church, Oklahoma City. But he was essentially an evangelist and he returned to his heart's work.

Ham considered himself a prophet-revivalist-evangelist. He attacked corruption and vice; he rebuked "professional" ministers and ministry for Christ; he mixed his method of presenting the message, "giving a little singing; then some preaching; then some more singing; then some praying; then some preaching," but always he exposed sin, warned of judgment, implanted conviction, called a disobedient people back to the truths they had forsaken and witnessed to *"a penitent and grieving people the good news of what Christ has done for them."*

A biographer, his nephew, Edward E. Ham, surely summed up Mordecai F. Ham's ministry with these words: "God raised up Evangelist Ham to do more than hold meetings in the great cities of the South. He ordained him a prophet to do more than lead great campaigns against liquor during the pre-prohibition days. God raised him up to remind Christian America of the main spiritual issue that has been in existence since man's beginning on this earth: Christ versus the Antichrist.

"Praying Hyde"

(1865-1912)

Men of God in our jet-set, space-race, big business-syndrome, swinging seventies are not especially known as men of prayer. Today's successful pastor, evangelist or missionary is more readily recognized as one who possesses charisma and charm; or, one who is an able administrator; or, one who is an outstanding organization man; or, one with Madison Avenue promotion power, etc. The reader will have to think tediously and tiringly to suggest the names of more than a couple clergymen who are characterized by their prayer life.

Perhaps that is why there is death and decay all about us in this day: shallowness in sermons, powerlessness in preaching, weakness in writings, mediocrity in music, lacklustre in Christian living.

Christian history has had its heroes of prayer: Elijah, the prophet whose prayers could turn off the faucets in the skies so it would not rain, then pray fire down from those skies and ignite revival on the altar of the idolatrous, iniquitous nation of Israel. There was the Apostle James, called "Mr. Camel Knees" because the flesh upon his knees had become calloused, hardened from his much kneeling in prayer. There was George Muller, who prayed in over seven and one-half million dollars and cited "over fifty thousand distinct answers to definite prayers" in over sixty years. Add the names Wesley, McCheyne, Hudson Taylor, etc.

But in these paragraphs I present to you another peer of prayer: "Praying Hyde." He was also called "the man who never sleeps," "the apostle of prayer," and many other titles of an intercessor.

PROFILES IN EVANGELISM

Well he might be, for, as Basil Miller wrote in his biography of Hyde:

> John Hyde was all of these and more, for deep in India's Punjab he envisioned his Master, and face to face with the Eternal he learned lessons of prayer which to others were amazing. Walking on such anointed ground. . .for thirty days and nights, or ten days on end, or remain on his knees for thirty-six hours without moving. . .when he returned to the field preaching from such seasons. . .he was thus possessed of a spiritual power which opened dark hearts of India to his message.

Such prolonged practice of prayer provoked his fellow missionaries to "awe, then disgust, finally to be filled with admiration for this apostle of intercession and to sit at his feet as disciples."

Hyde the missionary was, humanly speaking, a product of a preaching father and a couple of seminarians. In his Carthage, Illinois, pulpit, Hyde's father preached of "the ripened soul-fields into which the Lord of Harvest was to send forth laborers," and prayed from the pulpit and in the family altar that God would thrust out laborers into that field. His son, John, answered those pleas.

At McCormick Theological Seminary, Hyde surrendered to foreign missions. A stirring appeal by a fellow seminarian in chapel convicted Hyde. Not consummately convinced, he hurried to another seminarian, Burton Konkle. *"Give me all the arguments you have for the foreign field,"* he challenged. Konkle responded, *"You know as much about foreign missions as I do. Arguments are not what you need. What you want to do is go to your room, get down on your knees, and stay there until the matter is settled one way or another."*

Hyde did! The next morning, entering chapel, Hyde found Konkle and exclaimed, *"It's settled, Konkle!"* In the fall of 1892, after graduating in the spring, John Hyde set sail for Bombay, India.

Major crises immediately confronted him. First was the need of victory over selfish ambition and a full surrender to the Holy Spirit. That need was precipitated, for the most part, by a letter received from a friend of his father as Hyde boarded the boat. *"I shall not cease praying for you, dear John, until you are filled with the Spirit,"* were the words penned on the page. Hyde was incensed at what he considered a gross insult to his spirituality—but prayerful introspection revealed the accuracy of the accusation. Soon he settled all his selfish plans and purposes, confessed personal sins, and was assured of further victory and was "fully filled and dynamically conscious of the Spirit."

The second crisis was language. Hyde, handicapped with a slight deafness, found language study difficult. And rudely awakened to the fact he did not know his Bible sufficiently to "teach the dark-minded natives of Christ," he sacrificed language study for Bible study. Finally despaired, Hyde offered his resignation to the Synod. An appeal from the villages silenced that resignation and satisfied the Synod that Hyde should continue. The appeal read: "If he never speaks the language of our lips, he speaks the language of our hearts."

Hyde's work was an itinerant ministry in the many villages and progress was painfully slow and converts pitifully few. It was then that Hyde's intercessory prayer life began to mound the man, his ministry and, finally, his multiplied results. Hyde wrote of those days and nights of prayer:

> I have felt led to pray for others this year as never before. I never knew what it was to work all day and then pray all night before God for another. Early in the morning, four or five o'clock, or even earlier, and late at night to twelve or one o'clock, in college or at parties at home, I used to keep such hours for myself or pleasure, and can I not do as much for God and souls?

God's command in Isaiah 62:6, 7 became Hyde's personal prayer precept:

> *"I have set watchmen upon thy walls, O Jerusalem, which shall never hold their peace day nor night: ye that make mention of the Lord, keep not silence, And give him no rest, till he establish, and till he make Jerusalem a praise in the earth."*

90 *PROFILES IN EVANGELISM*

To obey that precept in prayer, Hyde missed meals, missed meetings, missed preaching appointments, but he never missed his meetings with God in prayer!

Revival came to India—iniquitous, idolatrous India—in 1904 at the Sialkot station. In Hyde's own ministry, he saw the years of no conversions multiply to fifty baptisms in 1907, 800 in 1909. In the 1910 conference, Hyde "was given assurance that his trophies for the year were to be four souls each day." Some of the most exciting evangelism tales in modern-day evangelism are told in the diary of that "diligent soul hunter" seeking sinners in the Punjab.

But in 1910, eighteen years after his entry into India, Hyde's intense prayer life and personal evangelism had taken their toll. His heart had shifted from its normal position—the doctors declared: months of quiet, or six months to live. Praying Hyde persisted in prayer knowing it meant a premature grave. *It did.* March 11, 1911, Hyde sailed for America—*to die.* He stopped in England, visiting Keswick and hoping to institute "a prayer room similar to the one at Sialkot." Then to Wales, where he visited Dr. J. W. Chapman, engaged in a great evangelistic campaign at Shrewsbury. Chapman invited that great intercessor to pray with him. Perhaps Chapman's commentary of that season of prayer best pictures Hyde in prayer.

> He came to my room, turned the key in the door, dropped on his knees, waited five minutes without a single syllable coming from his lips. I could hear my own heart thumping and his beating. I felt the hot tears running down my face. I knew I was with God.
>
> Then with upturned face, down which tears streamed, he said, "Oh, God!" Then for five minutes at least he was still again, and when he knew he was talking to God, his arm went around my shoulder, and then came up from the depths of his heart such petitions for men as I have never heard before, and I arose from my knees to know what real prayer was.

February 17, 1912, the man whom the Presbyterian Board witnessed was "one of the most devout, prayerful and fruitful missionary workers in India," ceased his intercession and evangelism with this triumphant

"Praying Hyde"

testimony as he died, *"Bol, Visu Masih, Ki Jah,"* —"Shout the victory of Jesus Christ!"

Need it be added—the number one need of our hour is a host of Hydes—men who will be "apostles of prayer" and evangels to the lost, the last and the least!

Quotes used above are from PRAYING HYDE by Basil Miller, Copyright 1943 by Zondervan Publishing House and are used by permission.

Dr. Bob Jones, Sr.

Dr. Bob Jones, Sr.

Evangelist

(1883-1968)

When Dr. Bob Jones, Sr., at the age of eighty-four years, laid down his robe of flesh, January 16, 1968, to "rise and seize the everlasting prize," Twentieth Century evangelism and education lost one of its most vital voices. For "Dr. Bob" was one of the few men, of any generation, who has been gifted of God with that rare balance of being an earnest, energetic and eminent evangelist and, at the same time, able to administrate one of the world's most renowned academic institutions.

Dr. Bob, born October 30, 1883, near Dothan, Alabama, began his ministry early. Assured of his soul's salvation at eleven years of age, he preached his first sermon at the tender age of thirteen *(although Dr. Bob fondly admitted that he used to preach to the children on Sunday afternoon in the woods when he was seven years old)*. When he was fifteen, Bob Jones conducted his first revival meeting, held under a brush arbor he helped to build. And, at sixteen years, Jones had even done some pastoring in some small Alabama country churches. And, for seventy years (some kind of a record, I am sure), Dr. Bob Jones preached.

"Preached" is the right word! For "Dr. Bob" was a preacher, one of the last of the "old-time evangelists"—men of the Finney, Moody, Torrey, Sunday stripe. It is estimated that Bob Jones preached face to face to more people than any person living. When he was only forty, Jones had delivered more than 12,000 sermons, had preached to over fifteen million people and had seen over

94 PROFILES IN EVANGELISM

300,000 come forward in his crusades to confess Christ. The mighty impact his ministry made for Christ is surely seen in this one campaign that could be multiplied manyfold—Montgomery, Alabama, his home when an evangelist. In that city of 40,000 population, the campaign averaged over 10,000 in attendance nightly, and many nights over one thousand came forward to make decisions for Christ. Recently the *Montgomery ADVERTISER*, in its 125th Anniversary edition, cited Jones' campaign in Montgomery over thirty-five years before "as the historical religious event of the 125 years' history of Montgomery." As Dr. Jones once sadly spoke: *"Most of the revivals we are having today are promoted and headlined, but back in the old days those revivals were not promoted—they made the headlines themselves."*

Aye—Dr. Bob Jones, Sr., was a preacher—a Christ-exalting, Bible-honoring, sin-condemning, sinner-converting, revival-producing preacher. Billy Sunday, contemporary with Jones, said of Dr. Bob: "He has the wit of Sam Jones, the homely philosophy of George Stuart, the eloquence of Sam Small and the spiritual fervency of Dwight L. Moody."

I was never privileged to hear any of those princes preach, but I thank God that I had occasions to hear Bob Jones. I first heard him when I was a Bible college freshman. That he was worth walking miles to hear is evident—I walked four or five miles nightly to sit under his ministry. His staccato-style, Spirit-of-God-filled, Scripture-relevant, soul-stirring sermons spoke to my heart! I was challenged, charged, yea, changed in that week's campaign. I am sure my service for the Saviour has been more meaningful because of the evangelistic influence of a Dr. Bob Jones.

But, as suggested earlier in this article, Dr. Bob Jones was more than an evangelist. He was an educator, too—a pioneer in the field of Christian education. *Not a monument* to his ministry in education, but a great movement that will ever enlarge his ministry, is the school of Dr. Bob founded forty years ago, now located at Greenville, South Carolina: BOB JONES UNIVERSITY, often called the *"World's Most Unusual University."* BJU is a plant worth an estimated thirty million dollars, annually has a student body approximating four thousand students, is the largest fundamental school in the world.

This miracle of God was begun by a man who never graduated from a college although Dr. Bob did attend three years at Southern University in Greensboro, Alabama. Sensing the shipwrecked faith among the youth of America because of compromise and liberalism in "so-called Christian colleges," Dr. Bob became burdened *"to build a school that would have high cultural and academic standards, and at the same time, a school that would keep in use an old-time country mourner's bench where folks can get right with God."* That was the beginning of BJU, "whose growth and influence have never been paralleled in so short a time in the educational history of America."

Behind every man's ministry is a philosophy. Dr. Bob Jones' philosophy is spelled out in the sentence sermons he has spoken to his "preacher boys" in BJU chapels, preached across pulpits and penned in the pages of his writings. Who has not heard or read some of these:

Duties never conflict.

The test of your character is what it takes to stop you.

You can borrow brains, but you cannot borrow character.

It is a sin to do less than your best.

The greatest ability is dependability.

Don't sacrifice the permanent on the altar of the immediate.

You and God make a majority in your community.

It is never right to do wrong in order to get a chance to do right.

The door to the room of success swings on the hinges of opposition.

A man who has no enemies is no good. You cannot move without producing friction.

Finish the job.

"DO RIGHT!" That was the philosophy that motivated

96   PROFILES IN EVANGELISM

his ministry, saturated his sermons, and spearheaded his
school. His voice has been silenced by death, but his
influence will ever exert his evangelistic and educational
impact across the nation and around the world in this
lawless and godless day through Christians who have been
challenged by him to "DO RIGHT IF THE STARS
FALL!"

Sam Jones

Evangelist

(1847-1906)

"One of the most fearless, sin-fighting evangelists that America ever produced" is the way one of his biographers introduced Sam Jones to his readers. And that he was! For Sam Jones was one of those worthies now only known as a memory in American religious history—the old-time, Hell-fire, circuit-riding, revival-producing Methodist preachers of the nineteenth century.

Jones, Alabama born (Cumberland County, October 16, 1847) but Georgia reared (Cartersville), joined the Methodist church at the age of seventeen. After a time of drifting in his spiritual life the young Sam Jones began a life of dissipation in drink. At the same time he began to study law, was admitted to the bar and soon became a success in his profession. Such success, however, simply sent him sliding deeper and faster into his dissipation. Marriage did not deter him from his drinking and it seemed sure that Jones would wind up in the damning destruction of the Devil's drink.

But a bedside repentance saved Sam Jones from the drunkard's doom. At his dying father's bedside, Sam promised his distraught dad, "Father, I'll make you the promise: I'll quit! *I'll quit!* I'll quit!" He said it in such determination and desperation that his dying dad had every assurance that his son meant it. *And Sam Jones did!* "He burned the bridges behind him, and walked away from that deathbed determined to live for the right." Jones *reformed* that day but he needed to be *reborn*. Groping for

Sam Jones

truth, help, strength, Sam Jones found it in an old-fashioned Methodist revival that was being conducted in Bartow County, Georgia, by his own grandfather.

Three verses of an invitation song had been sung after the sermon, and the weak, wavering Jones, afraid to go forward, said to himself,

I can but perish if I go
I am resolved to try;
For if I stay away I know
I must forever die.

Jones went forward and dated his conversion to Christ from that explicit experience. Years later he was to triumphantly attest: *"And I want to tell you, my neighbor, whatever else may be said, living or dying, I was a reformed, reborn, and changed man from that hour."*

Jones preached his first sermon one week after his conversion. His text was Romans 1:16. He was untrained in any theological school. He did not assume any pulpit manners or attitudes, nor did he attempt any analysis of his text, or give any attention to its unfolding. He adopted the philosophy of an old Methodist minister who reminded his hearers, "Brethren, I cannot preach the text, but I can tell my experience in spite of the Devil." God had saved his soul and Jones was not ashamed to tell the world. At the close of his earnest exhortation, he extended an invitation to that congregation. Many penitents came to the altar for prayer and were converted.

Soon Sam knew that he was to be a preacher instead of a lawyer. At the age of 25 he was licensed to preach. His wife had stood by him, suffered through his drinking days, but she stubborned herself against his desire to preach, threatening to leave him if he pursued his plan to become an itinerant preacher. The night before the conference when he was to be licensed, she became violently ill, repented of her resistance and at six o'clock the next morning awakened her mate to a hot Southern breakfast and saw him off on the train with her prayers.

The Methodists may have licensed Jones to preach but

PROFILES IN EVANGELISM

God had already called him. And God showed him through the preaching of another that a "preacher is not a vassal, not a slave, but a king and his throne is the pulpit." That message transformed the man and his ministry from that of a very "ordinary circuit-riding Methodist preacher" to one who was a straight-from-the-shoulder, hard-hitting, sin-rebuking, Spirit-of-God-energized, city-shaking evangelist.

Jones made no appeal to education, often attacking it. He could not tolerate stiffness, formality. His preaching was blunt, sometimes almost "uncouth." He had a stinging, sharp sense of humor with which he especially assailed hypocrisy in the church members. He was pungent, plain, pointed in his preaching, so much so that cooperating clergymen were often offended and outspoken in their criticism of Jones.

The late Dr. Will Houghton told the following story which well emphasizes the uniqueness of the evangelist:

> Jones was conducting a citywide revival campaign where great crowds were attending and many unsaved were turning to Christ. But the cooperating pastors felt Jones was preaching too negative sermons against sin—too little on love. And they felt he should be more dignified, use more tact, etc. So the pastors agreed to meet secretly one afternoon to pray for their evangelist.
>
> Quite by chance Jones came in about the middle of the prayer meeting. . .and was overjoyed to find the ministers conducting a prayer meeting. It did not take him long, however, to discover he was the object of their prayers. "O Lord, help Brother Jones to use more tact," prayed one pastor. "Help him to be more dignified in the pulpit," prayed another. "Change his mannerism," besought another. "Give him more respect for the clergy," called out another. . . .
>
> It was not until the last one prayed that they knew of Jones' presence. That was when he began to pray—"Lord, I hope you won't listen to a one of these preachers. They don't preach against sin, they don't visit door to door, they don't weep over sinners and they don't win souls. And they want You to change me until I'm most like them! O Lord, help these preachers to have sense enough to realize that if You were to answer their prayers I would be just as worthless and no account as

they are! Please God, don't make me like any of these fellers."

A group of very sheepish and subdued preachers listened as the evangelist went on to pray for a sweeping revival there—a prayer that God answered!

When Sam Jones died on a train at Perry, Arkansas, October 15, 1906, America lost a prince among evangelists, aye, a *"king whose pulpit was his throne."*

Adoniram Judson

Adoniram Judson
Father of Baptist Missionaries
(1788-1850)

By whatever measurement you measure the man Judson—the measurement always is the same—he was a mighty man!

Mentally—*he was mammoth.* He read at the age of three years, took navigation lessons at ten, studied theology as a child, entered Providence College (now Brown University) at seventeen—despite the fact he spent one year of his youth out of school in sickness—and he was a "veritable bookworm." Also, he mastered the Burmese language (possibly the most difficult language to acquire, excepting Chinese), writing and speaking it with the familiarity of a native and the elegance of a cultured scholar, and he also translated the Bible into Burmese. His biographers believe that his translation was "undoubtedly his greatest contribution to the people among whom he chose. . .to spend and be spent for Christ's sake."

Spiritually—*he was superlative.* Despite the fact his father was a Congregational preacher, and in spite of his mother's "tears and pleadings," Judson was not saved until he was 20 years of age. He had become a confirmed deist—due largely to the influence of a brilliant unbeliever in college who set out to win Judson to his deistic faith, and succeeded.

But, incredibly, Judson's conversion to Christ was due in large measure to that same deist. After graduation Judson left home to become a wanderlust. One night in a country inn his room was adjacent to the room of a dying man. The

104   PROFILES IN EVANGELISM

moaning and groaning of that man through the long night permitted Judson no sleep. His thoughts troubled him. All night questions assailed his soul: "Was the dying man prepared to die?" "Where would he spend eternity?" "Was he a Christian, calm and strong in the hope of life in Heaven?" "Or, was he a sinner shuddering in the dark brink of the lower region?" Judson constantly chided himself for even entertaining such thoughts contrary to his philosophy of life beyond the grave, and thought how his brilliant college friend would rebuke him if he learned of these childish worries.

But the next morning, when Judson enquired of the proprieter as to the identity of the dead man, he was shocked by the most staggering statement he had ever heard: "He was a brilliant young person from Providence College. E_____ was his name."

E_____ was the unbeliever who had destroyed Judson's faith. "Now he was dead—*and was lost! Was lost! Was lost! Lost! Lost!*" Those words raced through his brain, rang in his ears, roared in his soul—"Was lost! Lost! Lost!" There and then Judson realized he was *lost*, too! He ended his traveling, returned home, entered Andover Theological Seminary and soon "sought God for the pardon of his soul," was saved and dedicated his life to the Master's service!

His conversion not only saved his soul, it smashed his dreams of fame and honor for himself. His one pressing purpose became to "plan his life to please his Lord." In 1809, the same year he joined the Congregational church, he became burdened to become a missionary. He found some friends from Williams College with the same burden and often met with them at a haystack on the college grounds to earnestly pray for the salvation of the heathen and petition God to open doors of ministry as missionaries to them. That spot has been marked as the birthplace of missions in America.

Three years later, February 19, 1812, young Adoniram Judson, and his bride of seven days, Ann Haseltine Judson, set sail for India, supported by the first American Board for Foreign Missions. But on that voyage, Judson, while doing translation work, saw the teaching of immersion as the mode of baptism in the Bible. Conscientiously and courageously, he cut off his support under the Congregational board until a Baptist board could be founded to support him!

The Judsons were rejected entrance into India to preach the Gospel to the Hindus by the East India Company and after many trying times, frustrations, fears, and failures, they finally found an open door in Rangoon, Burma.

There was not one known Christian in that land of millions. And there were no friends in that robber-infested, idolatry-infected, iniquity-filled land. A baby was born to alleviate the loneliness of the young couple, but it was to be only for a temporary time. Eight months later, Roger William Judson was buried under a great mango tree. The melancholy "tum-tum" of the death drum for the thousands claimed by cholera, and the firing cannons and beating on houses with clubs to ward off demons, tormented the sensitive, spiritual souls of that missionary couple, too.

And there were no converts. It was to be six, long, soul-crushing, heart-breaking years before the date of the first decision for Christ. Then, on June 27, 1819, Judson baptized the first Burman believer, Moung Nau. Judson jotted in his journal: *"Oh, may it prove to be the beginning of a series of baptisms in the Burman empire which shall continue in uninterrupted success to the end of the age."* Converts were added slowly—a second, then three, then six, and on to eighteen.

But opposition came, also. Finally Judson was imprisoned as a British spy—an imprisonment of twenty-one months. Judson was condemned to die, but in answer to prayers to God and the incessant pleadings of his wife to officials (one of the most emotional-packed, soul-stirring stories in evangelism), Judson's life was spared and finally British intervention freed him from imprisonment.

PROFILES IN EVANGELISM

The work progressed and gospel power began to open blind eyes, break idolatry-shackled hearts and transform the newly-begotten converts into triumphant Christians. On April 12, 1850, at the age of 62, Judson died. Except for a few months (when he returned to America after thirty-four years from his first sailing), Judson had spent thirty-eight years in Burma. Although he had waited six years for his first convert, sometime after his death a government survey recorded 210,000 Christians, *one out of every fifty-eight! Burmans!* It was a partial fulfillment and a monument to the spirit and ministry of the man, who at Ava, the capital city, gazed at the temple of Buddha and challenged, *"A voice mightier than mine, a still small voice, will ere long sweep away every vestige of thy dominion. The churches of Jesus Christ will soon supplant these idolatrous monuments and the chanting devotees of Buddha will die away before the Christians' hymns of praise."*

Aye, a mighty man of faith, prayer, purpose, patience and perseverance for the Son of God and for souls, was Adoniram Judson!

Jacob Knapp
Evangelist
(1779-1874)

Rare will be the reader who will recognize the name of Jacob Knapp, and rarer yet will be the Baptist who will identify him as the individual who is considered to be the first of that now long line of elite worthies—*Baptist evangelists!*

It may seem very strange to our twentieth-century Baptists, who are so used to the evangelistic emphasis in our churches today, to learn that it was not until the first third of the nineteenth century that the first Baptist evangelist entered into the field of full-time evangelism. That was in September, 1833. And Jacob Knapp was the man.

As Dr. Frank G. Beardsley wrote of our early day Baptists in America:

> . . .aside from the Separate Baptists and Free Will Baptists, the Baptists as a class did not favor special efforts to promote revivals of religion. Since that would have been an interference with the operation of divine sovereignty it was considered presumptuous to undertake anything of the kind. The salvation of sinners was determined by God's elective grace and was to be accomplished independently of all human agency. . . .The strength of the church, therefore, was to "sit still!" This was largely the attitude taken by the Baptists when Elder Knapp began his labors.

Knapp was converted to Christ after the death of his mother. Although a member of the Episcopalian faith, the seventeen-year-old youth felt the "need of a comforter and friend this world could not afford, and to see the emptiness

108   *PROFILES IN EVANGELISM*

and vanity of all terrestrial enjoyment." Knapp underwent a prolonged period of soul-searching and praying into the late hours of the night that was relieved one Sunday morning in a woods when "his burden was suddenly lifted, and as he rose with uplifted eyes Christ seemed to him to be descending with open arms to receive him." Knapp dated his conversion to that hour.

Impressed that immersion was the scriptural mode of baptism, he was later immersed and united with the Baptist Church in Otsego, New York. Believing he was called to preach, Knapp prepared for the ministry at Hamilton Literary and Theological Institute, graduating in 1825.

He pastored two churches—Springfield and Watertown, New York. God gave great revivals under his preaching, so much so that Knapp was convicted and convinced God was calling him into itinerant evangelism. However the possibility of limited meetings and lack of finances posed a paramount problem to the young preacher.

Dr. Beardsley, quoted earlier, wrote of his victory thusly:

> He spent a whole day in prayer and fasting (which seemed to be an oft occurrence in his life) over the matter, continuing until midnight, when a sense of God's unseen presence came upon him and he seemed to hear a voice saying, "Hast thou ever lacked a field in which to labor?" He answered, "Not a day." "Have I not sustained thee and blessed thy labors?" "Yea, Lord!" "Then learn that from henceforth thou art not dependent upon thy brethren, but upon Me. Have no concern but to go on in thy work. My grace shall be sufficient for thee."

Knapp resigned at Watertown and entered evangelism. Suffice it to say, God provided for, and prospered the young preacher as He had promised. Knapp's early ministry was in his native New York with very successful campaigns in Albany (fifteen hundred converts), New York City, Brooklyn, Utica, Schenectady and Rochester. In New York City, the *New York Herald* sent a reporter to burlesque the meetings, but the strategy backfired and actually "brought multitudes to the meetings, many of whom. . .were led to confess Christ." From New York State, Knapp ministered in a wider circle of cities: Hartford and New Haven, Connecticut; Providence, Rhode Island; Boston and many other Massachusetts cities; Baltimore (where an estimated ten thousand professed conversion).

Knapp preached plainly, sharply on sin, especially gambling and drinking. As a result he had many exciting and, in this case, electrifying experiences. In Rochester, he announced he would "expose the secret orgies of a notorious gambling club in that city. About a thousand persons assembled in groups about the house of worship which was packed to suffocation." In Knapp's words:

> At three minutes before eight o'clock a stone came whizzing through the window towards the pulpit. Simultaneously with its passage came a flash of lightning, followed by a peal of thunder (this was in February, and snow was on the ground). In about a minute afterwards another stone came through the window accompanied by another flash of lightning, and followed by a still louder clap of thunder. Scarcely had another minute elapsed before another stone entered the building, when instantly the heavens pealed out their thunder more terribly than before. The house where the people were assembled was shaken, and the earth trembled beneath their feet. Fear seized the ungodly crew, and dropping their missles they hastened from the spot, as if they would hide themselves from the presence of God, lest He should "cut them off with a stroke."

Knapp was called the "Prince of Liars" in a letter from the gamblers in New Haven, who denied the thunder and lightning account and dared him to read the letter in his New Haven meetings. Knapp read it and Deacon Sage, a man who was present in Rochester, confirmed the truthfulness of Knapp's report. *"No sooner had he taken his seat than a sharp flash of lightning"* is reported to have *"blazed through the church, followed by terrific peals of thunder and torrents of rain."*

Some of Knapp's records read like the book of Acts. Not only did he witness divine interventions from Heaven, but he witnessed great revival results. He made a great

110 **PROFILES IN EVANGELISM**

contribution to the temperance movement, the famous "Washington Temperance Movement" resulting from his Baltimore meetings. But Knapp also made a most notable contribution to the cause of building up Baptist churches and engendering evangelism and revival spirit among the Baptists.

Baptists should rise up and call this man blessed, for Knapp, who died in 1874 in Rockford, Illinois, was the forerunner of the many, many soul-winning worthies called by the scriptural title of evangelists in our Baptist ranks today.

B. R. Lakin

A Conquering Caleb!
(1901-1984)

There are some amazing similarities between Caleb, the son of Jephunneh, and Bascom Ray Lakin. One similarity is seen in God's record of Caleb in Joshua 14:12, when the eighty-five-year-old warrior, who came out of the Egyptian bondage, survived Israel's wilderness wanderings of forty years, demanded of Joshua: *"Now therefore give me this mountain* [for his inheritance in the land of Canaan] *whereof the Lord spake in that day. . .if so be the Lord will be with me, then I shall be able to drive them* [the giants] *out, as the Lord said."* Those were the words of an eighty-five-year-old man who never lost his vision, his purpose of life, his courage and faith to believe God and his power to serve God!

B. R. Lakin is not eighty-five! He is still a "youngster" of only seventy-three! But with over fifty years of toiling, punishing ministry behind him, Ray Lakin is not about ready to settle down as a senior citizen to rest and relax. No, one thousand times, NO! There are mountains out yonder to conquer for the Lord, multitudes to reach for Christ, ministries to fulfill, miles to travel. His schedule is filled for the next few years in revival campaigns across the nation. B. R. Lakin has never been busier (he is averaging at least one invitation per day)—and I don't think he has ever preached better! Aye, like Caleb, B. R. Lakin is possessed of a perpetual vision, vitality of youth!

There is another cardinal characteristic of Caleb that shows up in B. R. Lakin. Caleb was not reminiscing sentimental words of a senile old man when he spoke of those eighty-five years of walk and warfare for the Lord,

B. R. Lakin

"Nevertheless my brethren that went up with me made the heart of the people melt: *but I wholly followed the Lord my God"* (Josh. 14:8).

That testimony is Ray Lakin, a man who never aspired to be and never expected to be more than a humble mountain pastor riding his mule to minister to his humble mountain people in his native West Virginia. And that's the way it began; but as Bascom Lakin wholly followed his Lord, God gave him a spiritual leadership that made him a prominent pastor, a renowned radio preacher, and now he has been elevated to the "loftiest reaches of evangelistic fame."

Lakin was a young teenage lad skidding logs out of the virgin forests of those West Virginia hills when he was converted to Christ. It was revival-meeting time in a little white, lop-sided church with its plain, pine flooring and a potbellied stove. Rev. J. C. Simpkins, "nephew of the legendary 'Devil Anse' Hatfield, one of the principal figures in the famous Hatfield-McCoy feud," was the preacher. It seemed to the young Lakin that every indictment, every word probed, pierced and penetrated into his innermost being with a sledgehammer force. Convicted, young "B.R." walked the aisle of prayer, and was "saved by the grace of God." A few days later the eighteen-year-old youth was baptized in Big Hurricane Creek.

Almost immediately God called the young convert to preach. Evangel Baptist Church, a little, humble, frame-structured, pot-bellied-stove-heated church in a way-out settlement called Greenbriar Creek, was his first charge. It was there young Bascom rode his mule to call on his members, seek sinners, and preach around the other settlements in the mountains. His "salary" was the sum of seven dollars monthly, to which Lakin laughs, *"I was the most overpaid preacher in the whole state!"*

Following pastorates were near Huntington, West Virginia; then Louisa and Prestonburg, Kentucky, on to Bristol, Virginia, where his strong, fundamental, doctrinal, premillennial-return-of-Christ messages, coupled with

114 PROFILES IN EVANGELISM

intense evangelism, doubtlessly were the weapons God used to spare that whole tri-state area from apostasizing to liberalism and modernism.

In 1939, Dr. Lakin became associate pastor of Cadle Tabernacle, Indianapolis, Indiana, and upon the death of Founder Dr. Cadle, became pastor of that once great edifice of evangelism that seated 10,000 and had a choir loft of 1,400. Lakin preached to over 5,000 on Sunday mornings and half that many on the Sunday nights were present. Cadle Tabernacle had no membership. It was a radio-preaching center and every day the only daily religious broadcast then coast-to-coast originated at the platform at 6:15 in the morning. WLW, Cincinnati, carried it at 50,000 watts one time to an estimated 800,000 listeners. Many readers will remember with not only nostalgia, but with converted souls, quickened lives and gratitude to God those broadcasts called "The Nation's Family Prayer Period." In those fourteen years, Ray Lakin became a household word across America.

In 1952, B. R. Lakin entered full-time evangelism. His ministry has carried him around the world, resulted in an estimated 100,000 decisions for salvation and legion the number entering the ministry—and who can count the churches and the Christians whose lives and testimonies have been quickened, strengthened and revived?

B. R. Lakin is a local church evangelist. His biographer, Kenny McComas, wrote: *"Churches are strengthened where he preaches. This primarily explains one reason he has always been reluctant to engage in citywide campaigns on a large scale. His love and devotion to the local church ministry exceeds the glamor and personal worship by well-meaning people which surrounds many of America's famous campaign evangelists today."*

"Preaching" is the right word to use of Dr. Ray Lakin. His messages are abrim with "wit, humor, pathos, burning compassion, pungent appeal." Dr. Tom Malone mentioned

what many, multiplied men believe about Bascom Ray Lakin:

> He has no peer as a preacher. He was gifted by God with a scintillating, brilliant mind and a masterful eloquence. . . .All of this talent has been completely dedicated to the service of the Lord Jesus Christ. I have often watched him take the Word of God and go to work on an audience as a skilled surgeon goes about his task. I have listened to him preach when it seemed a heavenly halo had settled about him. Then I have witnessed God putting his stamp of approval upon this man of God as multitudes came to be saved, and many lives have been blessed and changed.

It has been over fifty years since that Big Hurricane Creek conversion and baptism. There B. R. Lakin was called to preach. And there he began preaching the Gospel. He has ridden mules, cars, planes. He has preached to his original "18" high day at Greenbriar Creek. He has preached to the multi-thousands in auditoriums and over the radio. He has fought the battles for fundamentalism. He has known the toil of plowing, sowing and reaping in the harvest fields of sin, the work of which Dr. Noel Smith said, "There is no more work more spiritually, mentally, emotionally and physically exhausting." He has been molded by experience; by pain and sorrow and disappointment and loneliness; by a faith that sustained "when the stars have left the sky," but, like a conquering Caleb, Dr. B. R. Lakin keeps on climbing and conquering his mountains for Christ, for the churches, and for evangelism.

Paul Levin

Paul Levin

Evangelist

"Hello everybody!" Countless Christians across the country recognize that greeting from radio broadcasts, records and revival campaigns as the theme of Evangelist Paul Levin and his musical associate, Bob Findley. Well they might—for this team has been traveling the nation nearly forty years preaching and singing the Gospel of the Lord Jesus Christ!

Actually, Paul Levin has been a preacher longer than that. Paul points out that he believes he was called of God to preach even before he was born—just as the Prophet Jeremiah was. "I always had 'fire in my bone,' " Paul professes, adding, "Preaching is the one and only thing I really wanted to do in the Lord's work."

So, Paul started preaching at a precocious age—four or five years old. A piano stool for a pulpit, a few chairs for his audience, the tiny evangelist would exhort on Sunday afternoons—hollering, yelling, stomping in the mannerisms of his hero, his pastor, Fred Nelson—*only Paul Levin would sermonize in Swedish!* For Paul was born of Swedish parents, and English was an unknown tongue in the Levin home.

It was at the age of four Levin counts his conversion to Christ. There on the front porch of their Moline, Illinois, home, Paul's mother led her son to the Saviour. Like a Timothy, he had been tirelessly and truly taught the Word of God by his mother—so it was a real sinner who realized he was really lost who received Christ that day.

The fire in that boy's bones began to blaze for sure. As soon as he could read, Paul started to study the Scriptures.

118 PROFILES IN EVANGELISM

In school he would hurry to finish his lessons so he could read his New Testament, and Paul marked texts he hoped to preach some day. Reflecting, Paul philosophizes, *"How I thank God the Supreme Court hadn't gotten around to the deadly business of suppressing Bible reading and prayer in the schools."*

The fire faltered in Levin's life in his early teens, but a concerned mother's prayers for her son's cooling spiritual condition were answered. In a bed, flat on his back, in the Lutheran Hospital in Moline, the fourteen-year-old Levin learned one of life's supremest lessons: "He had better obey God!" Confessing his sin, Levin cried out to the Lord and claimed His cleansing. The fire in his bones surged into his soul. Paul Levin was going to be a preacher.

A few months later he was enrolled in a Bible High School Academy and, in January, 1930, age 15, Levin dedicated his life—all of it—to the Lord. Soon he was preaching for real, the first two years assisting his pastor-evangelist brother, A. H. Levin. At seventeen he was in full-time evangelism on his own and quite unbelievably, as a nineteen-year-old boy, he had engaged a full-time singer to accompany him—the blind, blessedly-used and honored-of-God Bob Findley. That was in 1934.

Yes, Paul Levin has been preaching quite a spell—*total: 46 years*. But let no one think that Levin is stodgy, getting senile, simply resting on his laurels. Although he is nearly twice the thirty-age mark, somehow set as a standard in the so-called generation gap, teenagers not only accept Paul Levin—the man and his message—they anticipate his ministry. This is evidenced by his record as teen-weeks evangelist for eighteen years at Bill Rice Ranch, Murfreesboro, Tennessee, and by youth attendances and decisions in his campaigns throughout the years.

Levin does all the preaching in the campaigns. Singer Bob Findley furnishes much of the music, although Paul accompanies him in duets. They use guitar, mandolin, piano and organ. Since the advent of rock music, Levin confesses that the congregations eye their mandolin and guitar suspiciously at first. But Levin and Findley are of the old school of evangelism in music, in message, in methods and in manners.

With a ministry spanning four decades, Levin is qualified to comment on evangelism, its philosophy and its future. Levin labels a lie the oft-heard alibi of the difficulty of reaching people today. He attests it has always been a struggle to get a crowd of sinners to gospel meetings, but he ardently adds, "Last year was the best year we have ever had and this year is the same, praise God." And Levin begs believers, *"I believe this is a great hour of opportunity, and all evangelists, pastors and Christians of sound, separated churches ought to go all out in soul winning, knocking on doors, extensive bus ministries, gear for evangelism, and forget all about 'why you can't have successful evangelistic meetings and why you can't see many people saved these days.'"*

Put it down—Paul Levin practices what he preaches about all-out effort in evangelism! Beside his church crusades, Paul and Bob minister on a daily radio broadcast over thirty stations that reach a great area of the nation. Paul is also president of Bible Tracts, Inc. He is the author of nearly forty titles, printed in over 230 million copies and translated in 76 languages. Converts to Christ through the tract ministry receive a personal letter from him, a free Bible correspondence course, encouragement and direction to a sound, separated, gospel-preaching church, and a copy of the booklet, *Safety, Certainty and Enjoyment.*

The reason for the booklet is Paul's concern that every convert be biblically assured of his salvation. That concern reflects the lamentable lack he experienced in his early ministry. Seeking help from Dr. William McCarrell, he was handed that booklet and challenged, "This is what you need to study." *And study it is what Levin did!* Levin relates, "The first time I thought it was good. The second time it was better. The third time it was better yet. The fourth time it was beginning to get through to me. The fifth time I hit the beefsteak, and the sixth time the brown gravy was running all over the place, and I learned the wonderful truth of assurance of salvation."

120 PROFILES IN EVANGELISM

But Levin learned more than that rock-ribbed, Bible-based guarantee of soul salvation that possessed his soul and has permeated his ministry—*it initiated him to the importance of literature distribution.*

Thus Paul Levin carries the torch of evangelism seeking to light fires of revival in this hour of confusion, compromise and complacency, when what was once condemned is now condoned, when the consciousness of sin is now collapsing. With strong Bible preaching against sin, strong praying to God, strong printing of the Gospel, strong singing the songs of the faith, Paul Levin, "born to preach," is still busy preaching! *Amen!*

Robert Moffat

Missionary

(1795-1883)

When I think of Robert Moffat, I am rightly reminded of the Scripture in Zechariah 4:10, which witnesses, *"For who hath despised the day of small things?"*

It seemed a small thing to some godly men in a Southern Scotland church when a boy about four years old, from a home of poor but pious parents, knelt at an altar to pray. His decision was despised by the elders as one who was too young to understand. Thank God, one unnamed, unknown-to-us brother bothered to kneel in prayer with "Robbie."

Moffat may well have been converted to Christ then—if not, it was the commencement of a chain of events that led to his conversion and to the opening of doors of evangelism to the uncharted depths of the dark continent of Africa.

In his mid-teens he left home for High Leigh, near Liverpool, England, to begin work as an undergardner. It was there that Moffat's spiritual convictions were confirmed and he became a member of the Methodists. And it was on a walk from High Leigh to Warrenton that another event occurred which would engineer him into evangelism in Africa. He saw a sign announcing a missionary meeting. On such a small thing as a poster, God prompted the heart of the youth to purpose to become a missionary. Moffat attended the meeting and there is every evidence he got the message for shortly afterward he contacted Rev. William Roby, the Methodist preacher in Manchester, and was soon recommended to the London

PROFILES IN EVANGELISM

Missionary Society. At the age of twenty-one Moffat reached South Africa.

His earliest ministries were treks taken into the interior. There were few railroads or roads and oftentimes those were washed away by rains. Travel was difficult, dangerous and often death-bringing. Rivers, rocks, swamps, forests had to be avoided or mastered somehow. Intense heat by day and chill cold by night complicated travel. Always there were the wild beasts: lions, jackels, hyenas, crocodiles, snakes, monkeys and, worst of all, warlike and untrustworthy native bushmen. Such journeys were not often undertaken by those who knew the country well, and to a newcomer like Moffat such treks were deadly dangerous! But Moffat, motivated by his missionary call, meant to master all such obstacles. He gradually became physically acclimated to Africa's extreme climates. He learned the country and became proficient in its customs and its languages, and he developed the great power of leadership that was to be his badge and make him a blessing to multitudes.

In 1817 he set out for the kraal, or village, of the Namaquas where the chief, Afrikaner, a blood-thirsty butcherer, was converted. That conversion has been considered one of the great accounts of the grace of God on the mission fields. On that trip he saw for the first time the Kurumon River and the Bechuanas, the peoples with whom he would spend most of his long missionary ministry.

The Bechuanas' reception of Moffat's ministry ranged from stony indifference—to steeled intolerance—to incorrigible rejection. Moffat, who had now married an English sweetheart, "saw no reward for untiring work." That work, by the way, consisted of being a builder, a carpenter, a smith and a farmer all in one; while at the same time preaching.

Probably one of the most momentous events in Moffat's ministry was not preaching but attempting to defend his Bechuanas from the warring Zuluas. He did not avert a war, but procured firearms and equipped his people. The Bechuanas conquered the Zuluas and, realizing Moffat's bravery and compassion in their behalf, they began to respect him as a friend.

It was twelve more years before his message bore the fruit of revival. Suddenly the meetinghouse was crowded. Heathen songs were not sung in the village and dancing stopped. Prayers came to the lips of the Bechuanas, and the songs of Zion were sung. They began to give up their dirty habits. Converts were recorded, then time-tested, then baptized. Other tribes, hearing the news, sent representatives to learn of the white man's teaching. Moffat often would return with them and thus the revival message and results spread.

It was then that Moffat realized he must concentrate on translating the New Testament into the language of the people if they were to learn God's Word and live God's way! And, customarily, he not only translated the text, he procured a press and printed it.

Moffat returned to England only one time before returning to die. On that visit he persuaded Livingstone to go to Africa instead of China. Livingstone built mightily upon the foundation that Moffat had so ably laid, yet, incredibly, Moffat outlived Livingstone ten more years.

He had opened jungle villages to the Gospel, he had braved the dangers, the deadlines of African jungles, he had withstood medicine men like Elijah had withstood the prophets of Baal at Carmel. He had preached, he had translated, he had instructed Africans to read, write, sing and farm. He had exalted Christ and magnified the ministry of a missionary. August 9, 1883, he wound his watch with a trembling hand. "For the last time," he said. And it was so. The next morning the 88-year-old soldier of the cross was dead, with eighty-four years of life for his Lord since that night as a four-year-old bairn (boy) he had come to Christ.

"For who hath despised the day of small things?"

Dwight Lyman Moody

Dwight Lyman Moody

Mr. Soul Winner

(1837-1899)

Occasionally there emerges a man out of the ranks of those soul-winning worthies called evangelists of whom it can rightly be said: "When God made him, He created a new mold and then broke the mold." This is altogether true of Dwight Lyman Moody. You can only explain this evangelist who shook two continents for Christ (America and Europe)—and who was one of God's greatest and the churches' chiefest evangelists; and who was one of times' supremest soul winners—by saying, "But God."

For if anyone ever appeared to be less qualified for the evangelist's office, it was D. L. Moody. He was unschooled (he quit after six years); he was unconventional (he refused ordination and rejected being called by any title except "Mr. Moody"); he was unseemly in appearance ("he was short, heavy looking—nearly three hundred pounds—commonplace man without grace of look or gesture"); he was unpolished and ungrammatical in his preaching ("his words rushed from his bearded face like a torrent; often two hundred and thirty per minute. . .short staccato sentences; imperfect pronunciation. Spurgeon said, "the only man I ever knew who said 'Mesopotamia' in one syllable; . . . .many 'aints' and 'have gots' ").

Yet Moody was a success in evangelism; aye, he was a superlative, even supernatural success. Of Moody, one is compelled to confess: *"He was an evangelist sent from God, for no man could have done the ministry he accomplished, except God was with him."* For in forty years Moody

126 *PROFILES IN EVANGELISM*

preached to over fifty million people, "Sweeping large communities into the evangelistic atmosphere and winning hundreds of thousands of souls to Christ." He founded the world-renowned and world-evangelizing Moody Bible Institute in Chicago, the Northfield schools in Massachusetts and the Moody Colportage Association which has ringed the world with literally millions of gospel messages and books. And, as one biographer appraised Moody's ministry:

> Probably his most lasting influence aside from his educational institutions lies in the direction of his influence over preachers and laymen in creating the soul-winning spirit and method. He, like Wesley, turned formal and unspiritual preachers and churches into soul-winning agencies. Moody will live forever in a class with Spurgeon, Wesley, Finney, W. A. Sunday, the world's greatest soul winners.

Soul winning! That is it! D. L. Moody was sold out to soul winning. In public or in private, in sermons and in songs, in lip and in life, Moody sought to save souls. Perhaps no one summarized it more succinctly than his son, William R. Moody, when he wrote, *"Father lived solely for the glory of God and for the spread of the Gospel of Jesus Christ."*

Indeed he did! His pressing, persistent plea to all his aides and friends, "Let everyone of us try to get one soul," pictures the passion, the purpose that pulsated in the heart and soul of this converted shoe clerk. And you believe it—*Mr. Moody practiced what he preached!* He determined that daily he would personally witness to at least one individual about his soul. *And he did!* His sermons read their richest and best where the stories of his personal soul winning are related. Buy a book of them. Read them. Let the soul-winning fervor and fire of Mr. Moody's mantle fall upon your ministry.

Which causes me to suggest that it would require a volume rather than a few pages to try to capture the spirit, the motivation, the methods and the messages of D. L. Moody that made him the master soul winner he was. But,

Dwight Lyman Moody

may I recount two epochal experiences in Moody's life that, I believe, started, shaped and sealed his ministry to become the soul winner he was by the grace of God.

First: *his conversion to Christ!* Moody was led to Christ by a personal worker, a soul-burdened Sunday school teacher who called on Moody while he was clerking at a Boston shoe store. Edward Kimball may never have won another soul to the Saviour, but that day, April 21, 1855—like an Andrew bringing a Simon Peter to the Christ; like an Ananias leading a Saul of Tarsus to the Light—Edward Kimball opened up a door of soul-winning evangelism that will never be closed until Christ comes back again to this earth. As I pen this paragraph, I pray, somehow, someway, may my every reader realize what portent, what possibilities, what potentialities for evangelism and for eternity are bound up in every call we make on pupils and prospectives.

The second transforming time was when Moody was a young Christian worker. It transformed him from being a man simply set out to become a millionaire merchant and to build the biggest Sunday school in Chicago, to become the man who would win souls around the world. A teacher in Moody's school, forced to resign his class of young ladies—because of incurable tuberculosis—and unsure of their soul's salvation, asked Moody to accompany him to visit each girl for the last time so he could present the plan of salvation to each one personally and press upon each the urgency of getting saved. Moody went.

He never was to be the same! Every girl "yielded herself to Christ." Moody then called the class together for a last prayer meeting before the teacher left for Michigan. In his own words, Moody witnessed: *"There God kindled a fire in my heart that has never gone out."*

That flame never flickered until Moody had to conclude his ministry in Kansas City and be carried back to his birthplace in Northfield, Massachusetts. There, on December 22, 1899, at the age of 62, Mr. Moody triumphantly testified on his deadbed: "Earth is receding,

Heaven is calling," and another of earth's choicest soul-winning saints went Home to receive his reward and to eternally experience Heaven's promise to soul winners: *"He that doeth the will of God abideth for ever"* (I John 2:17).

Henry C. Morrison

Evangelist

(1857-1942)

Meet Henry C. Morrison—one of the Southland's greatest sermonizers, one of the American pulpit's greatest preachers, and one of Holiness' greatest heralds. This is not simply a biographer's conclusion. No lesser an authority than William Jennings Bryan pronounced Morrison to be "the greatest preacher in the American pulpit." His friends fondly titled him "the Little Orator." Many are the men who believed Morrison had no peer as a preacher in his generation. Dr. Bob Shuler, fundamental Methodism's spokesman of the twentieth century and no slouch of a speaker himself, summed it thusly: "Not a man of his generation ever mastered the art of preaching more completely, or could hold great audiences with more the skill of a master. He was first and above all a preacher."

Aye, a preacher and an evangelist! That was Henry Morrison. As Shuler further stated, "He caught the meaning of the Master's command, 'Go ye, preach My gospel; disciple the nations.' Few men of all the history of the Methodist revival ever obeyed that command more effectively. . . .During his long and useful life, he was for many years a college president and the editor of a religious paper. But no fence was strong enough or tall enough to keep him in any pasture, however inviting. He was built for the range! He roamed at will across the nation, preaching—forever preaching! You would hear of him in Florida, in the Carolinas, in Tennessee, in Ohio, in California, in Oregon. If the world was John Wesley's

130   PROFILES IN EVANGELISM

parish then surely America was the pulpit for Morrison to continually plead with souls to come to Christ for full salvation."

Morrison was a Christmas-week convert to Christ. A thirteen-year-old youth, he was born again at a protracted revival meeting at the Glasgow circuit church of the Louisville conference of the old Methodist Episcopal South. Early in his childhood Morrison saw sin very real both in presence and power. The fear of God, the dread of judgment day and future woe and suffering, welled up in his heart. In great part that Holy Spirit conviction and constraint to call upon the Lord came as a result of the *"influence of a Sunday school superintendent's unctious prayers and his deeply solicitous concern for the lost, the messages of Brother Phillips, the Methodist circuit pastor and four Baptist preachers,"* Morrison mentioned. And he reflected further, *"These old men, in life and look, and sermon, made the things of God and the Bible fearfully real to a sinner. . . .I shall always be thankful that in early childhood I heard these men preach. There was nothing in their sermons to make one laugh, but with solemn faces, uplifted hands, and in thundering tones they cried out to men that they must repent or meet an awful judgment, and spend eternity in a waterless, bottomless pit of fire."*

Thus, that Christmas week, striving to seek peace for his sin-smitten soul, Morrison went forward to kneel at an old mourners' bench, but left night after night, "disappointed that God did not save him." His first appeal to the Lord for salvation was that "he was not nearly so outbreaking in sin as many other boys in the neighborhood and that he was an orphan boy (father and mother both died by his fourth year) and he thought this fact would certainly appeal to God's compassion." Each night the seeking sinner prayed in different vein his fears to quell, his soul to save. One night he sensed "he had made a great mistake in not offering to give God anything in return for pardon, so he made many promises of what he would do for God and His cause if He would only forgive his sins."

The night young Henry was saved he saw the scriptural truth of salvation and acted on it. In his own words, Morrison witnessed of that saving work in his soul: "I saw how sinful my life had been. He (the Holy Spirit) showed me the self-righteousness with which I had come to the altar. He showed me how I had tried to buy salvation by promising the Lord to do many things. He showed me how many times I had rejected Christ. . . .Up until that time I feared I might be lost. Now I clearly saw I was lost." Wailing aloud, sensing he was "sinking down, sinking down beneath God's righteous frown," Morrison was interrupted by a Baptist, Mr. Hammer, who assured the youth in tender tones, "God is not mad at you, God loves you; why, 'God so loved you that He gave His only Son to die for you.' " Inwardly Morrison sensed as if his soul said, "That is so; and in an instant he was on his feet praising God."

Morrison joined the Methodist church and became one of its mighty men, although because of his Holiness message "he was hounded and hunted, persecuted and misunderstood by the Methodism he loved." Morrison believed in a *"full salvation, and was never content with any salvation that was not full. A little, empty, selfish, worldly church member was the bane of his ministry. He knew how full Heaven is and he was always pleading with the people called Methodists to draw upon that supply."*

The story is hoary-headed with age. I have drawn it up from many writer's wells. But I share it with you in words written by Dr. Bob Shuler in his book, *I Met These on the Trail:*

"Dr. Morrison preached around the world and back just as Theodore Roosevelt arrived from one of his famous hunting trips. The great hunter was given a tremendous welcome at the landing. Dr. Morrison boarded a train and went down to Wilmore. For some reason nobody knew of his homecoming and no one met him. He walked up towards home, under the big trees that he loved and that make the campus at Asbury such a delight. He felt a little

132 *PROFILES IN EVANGELISM*

lonely and forsaken. How different from the welcome of a great hunter. I heard Dr. Morrison say that as he neared the college which he loved the thought came to him: Possibly I am not home yet.''

Morrison went Home in a revival meeting, collapsing on his way to the pulpit with a message burning in his heart. From the humble Kentucky home where his grandparents raised him, to Calvary by way of a mourner's bench in the old country church in Glasgow circuit, across the cities and the churches where he had preached to countless thousands, Henry Morrison that day was welcomed Home by a heavenly host of converts to Christ under his mighty and magnificent ministry and by the Christ who converted his soul, charmed his entire being, called him to preach, and created in him a champion of the pulpit and preaching!

Asahel Nettleton

(1783-1844)

I do not suppose many readers will recognize the name Asahel Nettleton. Time has a tremendous talent for dimming the luster of once greatly known lights in human history.

Asahel Nettleton! Who was he? To this man belongs the unique honor of being the "first native-born American to devote himself to the work of an evangelist." Yes, Asahel Nettleton was the first *American evangelist!*

Nettleton was converted to Christ during the Great Awakening of 1800, doubtlessly the most remarkable and righteousness-producing period of American history. (Without "protracted" meetings or "professional evangelists," revival fires were kindled and spread across the colonies of the newly-formed country.)

Nettleton was one of the converts. Connecticut-born (April 21, 1783), Asahel had been sprinkled as an infant and catechised in the Westminster Catechism by parents who were committed to "the half-way covenant plan." But Nettleton early sensed such was not sufficient for saving his soul. Once, when alone in the field, as he looked at the setting sun, he was deeply disturbed by the thought that he and all men must die. He was so moved that he wept aloud. But his earlier impressions were not lasting. At the age of seventeen years he was "overwhelmed" by the same thought that "we must all die and go to the judgment." Realizing his undone, unsaved, unprepared-to-meet-God condition, Nettleton gave himself to prayer, reading the Scriptures and religious books, even to writing "brief letters to some of his young friends, expostulating with them on

134 PROFILES IN EVANGELISM

their conduct." He often spent great periods in earnest prayer that "he would receive the forgiveness of sins together with the peace and consolation which God had promised to His people."

For ten months he wrestled with this state of conviction and its intermittent periods of "infidel doubts." But shortly afterward, Nettleton recognized *that a change in heart had taken place: his doubts were swept away. The character of God appeared surpassingly lovely, and Christ was exceedingly precious to his soul.*

Prior to his conversion, Nettleton had planned on "devoting his life to agricultural pursuits," but upon conversion to Christ he became deeply concerned "to be instrumental in the conversion of his fellow men," pledging himself "that if Providence should open the way, he would devote his life to missionary service." Upon graduation he was licensed to preach, but would not consider a call to a permanent pastorate because of his pre-determination to enter missionary service as soon as the providence of God should prepare the way.

But God never opened the doors to foreign service. So Nettleton spoke in pastorless churches and in the "most desolate unpromising places." He commenced his ministry in Eastern Connecticut, Massachusetts and New York, and his itinerant ministry continued with the great blessing of God until 1822 when Nettleton suffered a severe, almost fatal, attack of typhoid fever. He never fully recovered, although he continued to preach with evident success the remainder of his life, twenty-two more years.

Predecessor of Charles Finney by a few years, Nettleton never accepted "the new measure of revival and opposed many of Finney's methods, particularly, the anxious seat, praying for people by name, allowing women to pray," etc. Some of his biographers felt such oppositions were unfair, "because they seem to have been based upon misinformation due to exaggerated accounts which had been circulated by the opponents of Finney's work," and some felt that Nettleton's sickness "may have contributed to his distorted views of the matter." One writer, Dr. Edward Norris Kirk, simply stated of Nettleton, "I am informed that no revivals or evangelist in our day has so abounded in new measures, contrivances, and management as he."

Nettleton was not an evangelist of great eloquence, but he was a preacher possessed with great earnestness and preached with great power and persuasion. A sample of his sermons is seen in the excerpt by Dr. Bennet Tyler of South Britain, New York:

> As he arose, being an entire stranger, every eye was fixed upon him, and a breathless silence pervaded the assembly. With great solemnity he looked round upon the congregation, and thus began. "What is the murmur which I hear? I wish I had a new heart. What shall I do? They tell me to repent. I can't repent. I wish they would give some other direction." He thus went on for a short time, personating the awakened sinner, and bringing out the feelings of his heart. He then changed the form of his address, and in a solemn and affectionate manner, appealed to the consciences of his hearers, and showed them they must repent or perish, that it was their reasonable duty to repent immediately and that ministers could not direct them to anything short of repentance, without being unfaithful to their souls.

Such preaching produced repentance and revival results. Dr. Noah Porter, Farmington, Connecticut, wrote:

> The state of feeling which, at the time, pervaded the town, was interesting beyond description. There was no commotion; but a stillness in our very streets; a serenity in the aspects of the pious; and a solemnity apparent in almost all which forcibly impressed us with the conviction that in very deed, God was IN THIS PLACE. Mr. Nettleton continued with us, except during a few short intervals, till about the middle of April. To his labors, so far as human instrumentality was directly concerned, the progress of the revival must be ascribed. . .his addresses. . .were too plain to be misunderstood, too fervent to be unheeded, and too searching and convincing to be treated with indifference.

Some of his revivals were far-reaching. One campaign in

136   PROFILES IN EVANGELISM

1819 was commenced in Saratoga Springs, New York, while he was recovering from illness. The revival spread to Malta, to Schenectady and to the countryside round about. The entire region was profoundly moved, upwards of two thousand conversions being reported.

The frail, sickly, tubercular man who died, May 16, 1844, is practically an unknown name in America today. But he was the first of that illustrious group of soul-winning worthies called evangelists who blazed trails with the pioneer settlers across trackless wildernesses, who journeyed into the isolated and wayside communities, who shook cities and helped preserve the spiritual and moral life and soul of our nation.

May his and their tribe increase!

Sam Raborn
Gospel Singer

I don't think anyone forgets his first meeting with Sam Raborn! I'm sure I won't!

Leaving my "prophet's chamber" to enter the church for my first service in a revival with the Eastview Baptist Church in Tucson, Arizona, a tall, Texas-hatted, well-groomed gentleman extended his hand and boomed, "HOWDY! I'm Singing Sam Raborn—that's spelled R-A-B-O-R-N! When you're from Texas, and over six feet tall, there's no 'y' in the name. R-A-B-O-R-N, the Texas Gospel Baritone."

I had heard of "Singing Sam"—now I had met him. He was to sing in some of those meetings and during those days I was to get to know the man as well as his music. Suffice it to say, my ministry is much richer because of it.

Sam is an old-timer—"seventy-six years young," he admits, but he attests his voice is only "fifty." And I accept it as fact, for when Sam sings "The Golden Bells," his favorite, or, "How Great Thou Art," or, "The Old Rugged Cross," among the hundreds of songs in his repertoire, no one would slightly suspect they were listening to a man who has been singing for Jesus fifty-six years.

Sam comes by his voice naturally, although he is first and fast to recognize that his melodious baritone voice that reminded Mrs. John Charles Thomas of her own son's trained and tremendous voice is a gift of God. Sam's father was a well-known gospel singer and evangelist, and his mother had a voice like Kate Smith. Sam inherited the ability and beauty of both parents' voices.

The Hillsboro, Texas-born Raborn was saved as a

Sam Raborn

twelve-year-old boy in a revival campaign. In those days, public schoolteachers would dismiss pupils from classes to attend the morning revival services. And Sam attended and was saved. His family shortly moved to West Virginia and, as a young man, Sam began to sing for his father in revival meetings. During those days he met and ministered with Evangelist T. T. Martin, the man who probably had the most influence in the young singer's life. But doubtlessly the outstanding event that prepared him for his life's work as a gospel singer was an incident that occurred in Camp Lee, Virginia. A corporal, soon to be commissioned to be an officer, Raborn volunteered one day to tend a host of men sick and dying of the flu. It was a mission more dangerous than facing German bullets, Sam reflects. His chaplain, arrested by his compassion and attracted to his ability to minister to the men, sought him to forsake the commission and assist him in the music ministry. Raborn accepted the challenge of the gospel ministry.

"Singing Sam" has sung for many of the greatest preachers of this century: Billy Sunday, Dr. R. A. Torrey, George Truett, Edward Biederwolf, and others.

And he has had a radio ministry. Some older readers of this volume will remember "Singing Sam" as the soloist on the Wheeling Steel Hour, NBC coast-to-coast network. He also had a twelve-year broadcast over Beckley, West Virginia, and for many years broadcast with Dr. Dale Crowley in Washington, D. C.

He was voted the West Virginia American Legion Convention soloist for life, a position from which he eventually resigned because of the Legion's refusal to take a stand against booze, etc.

And Sam has preached—in churches across the country, in revivals, even in prisons. But Sam is most at home singing!

His philosophy is that the gospel singer's purpose is to inspire and not to entertain. This conviction crystalized in Tampa, Florida. Dr. R. A. Torrey was the speaker.

PROFILES IN EVANGELISM

"Singing Sam" was the soloist. In deference to the great doctor to give him all the time possible, Sam sang only two verses of "Somebody Cares." At the conclusion of the song, Dr. Torrey arose and spoke to Sam, "Isn't there another verse to that hymn?"

Sam said, "Yes, Sir. But I did not want to take your time because I know the people want to hear you speak."

Torrey replied, "But my soul needs inspiring also, and that song thrills my soul, so come back and sing the other verse."

Sam's singing inspired one of the most beloved hymns in our hymnals, "Why Should He Love Me So?" Sam had finished a solo at the Southern Baptist Convention songfest, "He Will Not Let Me Fall." The Australian pianist and composer Robert Harkness said to Sam, "How is it you can sing while I can not carry any kind of a tune?" Sam suggested, "Bob, I cannot tell you why God loved me so. But He called me and gave what voice I had to sing gospel hymns and through them to tell the story." The phrase, "why God loved me so," spoke to Harkness's heart. In a few minutes he composed the music and the message of one of his greatest hymns.

Aye, "Singing Sam" uses his gift from God *"to sing the message of God and to tell the story of Jesus to the people. And to sing with the Spirit and understanding since a gospel singer is called to inspire people and not to entertain people."*

Sam Raborn is probably the last of his generation of gospel singers. He bridges the gap of nearly six decades. Yet I noticed the youth as well as the oldest listening intently to this old-time, old-fashioned gospel singer. There is no generation gap when "Singing Sam" speaks out the words of wisdom he has picked up through the years, or when he sings out for his Saviour.

A younger brother recently chided Sam that he ought to retire and settle down before someone asks him to quit! But Sam is not about to retire. With his wife, he now lives in Tucson, but Sam is constantly on call from churches across the country—people who want their hearts warmed and their souls stirred by the man and his music.

I well remember Sam's saying in one service, "Every time we make a friend we grow a little." Aye, altogether true when you make a friend of "Singing Sam" Raborn. I know. I met him and ministered with him.

Bill Rice

Bill Rice
Evangelist
(1912-1978)

Some servants of the Saviour make a striking, significant impression on you the first time you meet them or hear them minister. *Bill Rice is one of those noteworthy men.*

I first heard Bill Rice at a chapel service when I was a student in Bible college. You can be sure not all chapel speakers were exciting, enthusiastic, attention-getting and attention-holding platform personalities to the students who labored long hours in classes over doctrine, history, Greek, etc.

But Bill Rice registered! *"Howdy neighbor,"* he drawled with a western accent native to his West Texas birthplace in the little cowtown of Dundee. And then, in what seemed to be one of the briefest chapel periods I can remember, Bill Rice made the Scriptures speak to our souls in his homespun way, his gripping stories and his warmhearted understanding of his audience. Aye, when Bill Rice finished his message I knew I had heard a preacher of the Gospel!

Since that day back in the mid-forties, Dr. Bill Rice has become a man with a multi-faceted ministry. He edits a Christian cowboy paper, *The Branding Iron,* manages a conference ground, conducts the world's largest missionary camp for the deaf—registering campers from twenty-eight states last summer (the Rices' interest in the deaf resulted from an illness which left their oldest daughter deaf when she was just a child). And "Dr. Bill" is also co-editor with his brother, "Dr. John," of *The Sword of the Lord,* the largest evangelistic weekly paper in the world. He also

144   *PROFILES IN EVANGELISM*

conducts a weekly radio broadcast and serves on several mission boards. But with that busy schedule he is still a full-time evangelist and with all those multiplied ministries Bill Rice is still *first, foremost,* and at his finest—a preacher!

Rice remembers his call to preach by relating, *"When I was nineteen years old I 'surrendered to preach.' There was no question in my mind but that God had called me to preach. The Lord, however, had forgotten to call anyone to listen to me preach."* But Bill preached: on street corners, to transients in railroad depots, hitchhiking from place to place and sleeping under bridges and in haystacks.

After a year of such ministry, Bill received his first invitation to preach in a church—and at a fellowship meeting! The kids were dismissed after lunch to go and play, the women cleaned up the tables and the pastor mentioned to the men, "Of course, some of you men may want to smoke for awhile instead of coming in the church and hear Brother Bill Rice." But Rice relates, "Oddly enough, I was honored more than I knew how to say. For the first time in my life I had been invited to preach in a real church with electric lights and everything just like uptown! What's more, the pastor had called me 'Brother Rice.' That in Texas, means *preacher!"*

He received no offering, no one invited him to spend the night in his home, and he walked back to the bridge where he had slept the night before. But he was happy—he was recognized as a preacher! Soon he began getting invitations to preach and from that day on he has had more invitations for revivals than he can accept.

During those early days of ministry Rice worked his way through a Baptist college in Texas and then moved to Chicago to attend Moody Bible Institute. After graduation he became a staff evangelist for the Institute and then, in the late forties, Bill Rice became an independent evangelist and has conducted revival campaigns from coast to coast and overseas.

As his wife has well written, "Whatever life has been for Evangelist Bill Rice it certainly has not been dull."

Decidedly not when you consider that "Bill" was breaking broncos and wild horses at the age of thirteen—has become an experienced airplane pilot—has built a great Christian ranch in Murfreesboro, Tennessee (where he now makes his home with his wife and two evangelist sons: Bill, III, and Pete)—has hunted big game in Africa. One time "with two Bibles, two six guns, two cameras, and accompanied by two white companions, Rice plunged into an uncharted African jungle where they located pygmies and made a missionary contact that resulted in one of the few organized pygmy churches in the world. Add to those thrilling times the fact that Bill Rice was one of the last Americans to visit the late King Abdullah of Palestine before the monarch was murdered. "The Bearded Lion of Judah" was so attracted to the evangelist that he made him a present of two of his finest Arabian horses—and this in spite of the fact that Rice had warned him, he would surely go to Hell if he did not receive Christ as his Saviour.

Aye, life surely has not been dull for Bill Rice. Neither is his preaching dull to his hearers. Carefully and tellingly woven into his messages are stories out of his eventful life as cowboy, collegian, aviator, world traveler, evangelist and soul winner. And always warming his message to his hearer's heart is the winsomeness and the warmheartedness of a man who closes each correspondence, *"With a warm handshake, Yours in Christ Jesus, Bill Rice."*

In recent years, in citywide and local church campaigns, Rice has conducted his meetings with a six-person team. Jim Stoutenborough is promotion man and song leader. Dr. Billy Renstrom is team soloist. Before the evening service, Dr. and Mrs. Renstrom and Mrs. Stoutenborough conduct a one-hour children's program. Mrs. Bill Rice—"the Princess," as Bill affectionately calls his wife—conducts a class on marriage. Then "Brother Bill" Rice preaches!

And in Texas—or anywhere in the world, "Brother Bill" Rice means "a preacher!"

John R. Rice

John R. Rice

Evangelist

(1895-1980)

Probably no evangelist living today has had a more profound influence on evangelism in America in this generation than the subject of this article, Dr. John R. Rice. Probably more than any other one man, Dr. Rice has been instrumental in igniting revival fires again in America, in inspiring Christians—both pastors and people—to individual witnessing and soul winning, and in encouraging the cause of New Testament evangelism.

Lest someone think those statements are untenable—simply sentences of superlatives—consider some of the singular successes Dr. Rice has realized in his service for the Saviour.

Dr. Rice has been considered one of America's leading soul-winning evangelists and revival exponents since 1926, a sustained period of fifty years. Along with his successful campaigns that have revived churches, resulted in new churches, and wrought great victories in such citywide campaigns as Akron, Ohio; Binghamton, New York; Buffalo, New York; Cleveland and Chicago; among many others; Dr. Rice has edited *The Sword of the Lord*, rightly recognized as America's greatest soul-winning magazine, since 1934. This sixteen-page weekly, which regularly features two or three full-length sermons—at least one by one of the great preachers of the past, and one by a great gospel preacher of the present day—plus an arsenal of articles on vital issues of the day, answers to questions, "Incidents and Illustrations" by Dr. Bob

148 PROFILES IN EVANGELISM

Sumner, etc., now totals nearly three hundred thousand subscriptions going into every state and about one hundred foreign countries. Thousands of pastors and missionaries receive *The Sword* which has been described by one nationally-known evangelist thusly:

The paper breathes devotion to Jesus Christ, compassion to the souls of men. Each issue is a blazing torch of fire, enough to set aflame the heart of the coldest, the most backslidden Christian and the fartherest-away-from-God sinner.

It is small wonder, then, that most soul-winning pastors and evangelists regularly read this ministry-transforming, zeal-inspiring, soul-refreshing paper. Suffice it to say, that although not everyone will agree with every article, every answer, every argument of the editor and the contributors, my own personal conviction is that *The Sword is* and *has been* one of the mightiest means in our day to light revival fires and stir God's people to purpose and passion and power in personal evangelism!

Another incalculable contribution to rekindling revival fires in America is the Conferences on Evangelism which Dr. Rice inaugurated back in the "forties." When evangelism and revival in America were considered impossible and passe, Dr. Rice, one morning at two o'clock in a southside Chicago YMCA, discharged the burden on his heart by definitely committing himself to God to bring back mass evangelism and citywide campaigns to America.

One of the methods God led him to was such conferences. The first was held in Chicago. *"People came from Illinois, Indiana, Wisconsin, Michigan, Iowa, Missouri, Texas, Kansas. Great good was accomplished and other conferences followed."*

It was in such a conference, Thanksgiving week, in 1948, that my visions were lifted, my motives enlarged and my life surrendered to major my ministry in evangelism and revival. Many, multiplied are the men I have met in the fundamentalist ranks who have had their ministries transformed in similar conferences.

Another real contribution of **Dr. Rice** to revival is his writings. He has a prolific pen. Over 60 million copies of his books and pamphlets "have been **gotten** out by the Sword of the Lord Publishers." This would include over 150 full-length volumes of sermons and studies. Some are considered classics, particularly, *PRAYER—Asking and Receiving,* the world's best seller on prayer! His paperback pamphlets and his multi-language-translated tract, *"What Must I Do to Be Saved?"* have helped account for 17,000 letters from people who wrote to say they had trusted Christ through Sword literature.

Dr. Rice and his ministry are colorful (born in Texas, Cooke county, December 11, 1895, Rice has often been called the Will Rogers of the pulpit). And his ministry has been controversial. Controversies—and correctly so—have been carried on against the modernism and socialism of the National Council of Churches, the World Council of Christian Churches, infidelity in denominational colleges and seminaries, the Revised Standard Version, the Interpreter's Bible, the Bishop Oxnams, Harry Emerson Fosdicks, Nels Ferres, etc.

And added to that could be the "position he has taken with the Billy Graham crusades, and error when it has cropped up in conservative circles."

Dr. Rice is a man of convictions, intense convictions. To some, many of Dr. Rice's issues are comparatively unimportant, but to Dr. Rice an issue is never unimportant and he speaks out uncompromisingly, dogmatically, boldly, regardless of the personality or the price involved. *But Dr. Rice is also a man of compassion.* He is a man who can weep over sinners and weep with the saints. I know! I have had the high honor of ministry and fellowship with him!

Dr. Bob Jones, Sr., founder of Bob Jones University, wrote, "I regard Dr. Rice as one of the greatest spiritual assets this nation has." Many other men in America would agree with that appraisal.

Evan Roberts

Evangelist

(1878-1950)

When the roll call of the great religious revivals is fully complete, one of those written in that record will undoubtedly be the Welsh Revival of 1904. Gipsy Smith called it the "Acts of the Apostles up-to-date," and accurately added, "[It] ought not to be called 'The Welsh Revival,'. . .for I believe it will shake England, and why not the world?" Dr. George T. B. Davis described his thoughts, "This is a picture of what must have occurred in the early church in the first century of the Christian era." Mr. W. T. Stead, editor of *Reviews of Reviews,* wrote back to London, declaring in all seriousness that "he could find no trace of the Devil in Wales at the present time."

The Devil had not really disappeared, nor had he been destroyed by that revival, but that he had been soundly defeated was undeniable! Theater-going dropped drastically. All across Wales, talented actors and actresses failed to draw any sizable attendances. Foolish jests about the revival indulged in by comedians not only fell flat, but aroused indignation. In one village the entire football team disbanded because its members had been converted. Soccer and rugby matches were cancelled or rescheduled. Dance halls in area after area were completely deserted. "Young women cut up their expensive frocks of which they had been proud, thus making sure they would not succumb to any luring temptations." At Aberdare, Christmas Eve was almost free from any drunkenness, and "on Christmas Day there were no prisoners at all in the cells." The Abercarn (a city of 21,000) Police Court did not issue a single summon one day, something unknown in fourteen years of operation. Reports vary, but in a few months seventy thousand to one hundred thousand were said to have been saved, baptized and added to the churches.

Probably one of the greatest transformations was seen in the speech of the Welsh miners. These men were marked by their profanity and blasphemy. But Satan-possessed tongues were converted to Christ and their profanities gave way to paeans of praise sung or spoken to the glory of God in the lilting beauty of the Welsh brogue.

Humanly speaking, Evan Roberts was the individual that ignited that flame of revival that spread like a forest fire through collieries, cities, aye, the whole country. Roberts was only twenty-six years old, a student in preparatory school for the ministry, when the revival erupted. He had been a collier, and later had been apprenticed to become a blacksmith when he felt called to preach.

He was born in Loughor, a small village near Swansea, and dated his salvation to an evangelistic campaign conducted by Seth Joshua. Roberts had first attended the campaign at the insistence of his grammar school principal. Impressed by the definiteness and fervor of the evangelist, Roberts followed him to the next campaign at Cardigan Bay. In a service where he was experiencing unusual difficulty in preaching, Joshua prayed at the conclusion of the message, *"Bend us—bend us—bend us, O Lord!"* Many believe the Welsh revival began at that utterance of that sentence because it had a profound place in Robert's conversion and was used again and again in his messages.

He commented on his conversion, *"I would have burst if I had not prayed. What boiled me was that verse, 'God commending His love.' I fell on my knees with my arms over the seat in front of me, and the tears and perspiration flowed freely. I thought blood was gushing forth. For about two minutes it was fearful. I cried, 'Bend me! Bend me! Bend us!. . . .What bent me was God commending His*

152 PROFILES IN EVANGELISM

love (Romans 5:8), and I not seeing anything in it to commend. After I was bent a wave of peace came over me, and the audience sang, 'I hear thy welcome voice.' And as they sang I thought of the bending at the Judgment Day, and I was filled with compassion for those who would be bent on that day, and I wept. Henceforth the salvation of souls became the burden of my heart. . . ."

This crushing, consuming concern finally caused Roberts to cease his studies and go and tell family and friends the burden of his soul. For thirteen months he had been sighing and crying out to God for a great spiritual awakening for his beloved Wales. He went home and the fires of Heaven fell!

His ministry began with the youth in his boyhood church. A crowd came out of curiosity. Roberts bared his soul. "The hours passed unobserved, tears flowed, youth bowed in prayer, some sang, others spoke of their salvation, many testifying for Christ for the first time." David Matthews, in his book, *I Saw the Welsh Revival,* witnessed of that meeting, "It did not break up until midnight with happy youth singing Psalms. The next day the village was agog. . . .The chapel was not closed afterward night or day for many months."

At first, Roberts stayed in his native Loughor, albeit, even there he had little time to sleep, eat, drink, or change clothes. For the slight-built, medium-height, brown-haired youth it was day-and-night ministry in music, prayer and exhortation. In his own meetings Roberts led the music, did not preach, but exhorted before and after verses in songs, and led in testimonies and in prayer. Foul-mouthed miners, drunkards, sinners of every stripe, hardened youth, who had previously withstood earnest messages of eminent preachers became converted in these meetings. Then glowingly, gloriously, they would testify of their newfound faith. Some spoke, some sang as the Lord led them in spontaneous expression. It was in this respect the Welsh revival is without precedent. It was not so much a revival through powerful preaching by preachers as by a plenitude of lay people! The revival continued unabated and unchecked as a roaring fire for many months.

Evan Roberts must have realized then and remembered up to his dying days an incident that predicated that revival. When he was still a collier, an explosive fire swept through the mine. Roberts escaped unhurt, but the leaves of his Bible were scorched by that fiery blast. Strangely enough, the Bible was opened to II Chronicles 6, where Solomon's prayer to God for revival is the price Evan Roberts and many other revival-burdened Welshmen paid for that revival that swept Wales in the early 1900's.

Seventy years have passed. We need a similar visitation from Heaven. Who will pay the price of importunately pleading, petitioning Heaven that revival fires will fall again and God's people will rejoice in Him (Ps. 85:6)?

Ira David Sankey

Ira David Sankey

Music Evangelist

(1840-1908)

For a hundred years the name of Sankey has been synonomous with evangelism—especially musical evangelism. For when Sankey became co-laborer with D. L. Moody, he began a career that would cause him to be called *"the gospel singer in the greatest services of evangelization put forth since the apostolic times."*

The way the Moody-Sankey association came about is a classic story in Christian circles. At a morning prayer meeting of the YMCA in Indianapolis, the congregational singing was dragging along in a woeful way. Sankey, who was a delegate, was seen in the audience and asked to assist. The immediate upsurge in spirit and singing attracted the attention of Mr. Moody, who in his straightforward New England way asked Sankey, "Where do you live?"

"In New Castle, Pennsylvania."

"Are you married?"

"Yes."

"How many children have you?"

"One."

"I want you."

"What for?"

"To help me in my work in Chicago."

"I can't leave my business."

"You must. I have been looking for you for the last eight years. You must give up your business and come to Chicago with me."

PROFILES IN EVANGELISM

Sankey promised to pray about it. He did. And he went. Thus the musician who had never had a professional lesson in his life—and had publicly attested that he could not distinguish between the tunes of "Old Hundred" and "Yankee Doodle"—became partner with D. L. Moody in evangelism in Chicago.

But the Pennsylvania-born Sankey (Edinburg, Pennsylvania, August 28, 1840) was to minister in music more than in Chicago. His evangelism was to be enlarged to include America, Scotland, Ireland and England. By the way, it was in Scotland that Sankey's classic song, "The Ninety and Nine" was born. Sankey had clipped the poem out of a religious weekly, *The Christian Age,* and one night after Mr. Moody had preached on the subject, Sankey reportedly composed the music to the poem as he played it for the first time as an invitational number. It became one of his favorite hymns, as well as a favorite of all Christendom.

Sankey's music shook Scotland like a storm. The Scots, reared on "Rouse's rugged version of the Psalms," were quick to ostracise any hymn or spiritual song as "uninspired" and were prejudiced against all use of musical instruments in the sanctuary. However, they were immediately captivated and captured by Sankey's melodeon and melodies. Doubtlessly, his sympathetic voice, his joyous spirit and his "hymns so inwrought with grace and truth" were factors that won the cautious, suspicious Scots "almost on sight." The demands for his music in printed form were so great that Sankey compiled his famous *Gospel Hymns* and *Sacred Songs and Solos,* of which over fifty million copies were sold around the world.

Sankey was not only a soloist and a composer and a choir director, he was a song leader "who taught the people of his generation to sing and make melody in their hearts unto the Lord." Much of our present-day emphasis and enjoyment of evangelistic music in revival campaigns and our Sunday services had its origin in the brain and breast of Ira David Sankey.

When he died in 1908, he left us a rich heritage of music. Besides the "Ninety and Nine," Sankey composed such favorite gospel music as "Faith Is the Victory," "Trusting Jesus," "A Shelter in the Time of Storm," "Hiding in Thee," "When the Mists Have Rolled Away," etc.

A convert to Christ in an evangelistic campaign himself at the age of fifteen in his native Pennsylvania, Sankey gave of himself largely and liberally in time, talent and treasure to the cause of winning souls to Christ. The Great Awakening of the Nineteenth Century came about in large measure through great gospel *preaching*—but it also came about in great measure from great gospel *singing*. As much as any one man, Ira David Sankey was the evangelist of music.

Girolamo Savonarola

Revivalist

(1452-1498)

This profile is no attempt to appeal to, nor to appease, nor to propogate ecumenical evangelism. Savonarola was a Roman Catholic, a friar, a monk in that faith; but he was a real revivalist, a reformer and, finally, a martyr for his stand against sin.

Savonarola was born in Ferrara, Italy, September 21, 1452, "when Catholicism from its pope, its princes to its people had sunk to its lowest in cruelty and corruption." *"For long the popes had contemptuously thrown aside the pretense of piety; they were not only privately vicious, they were openly and blasphemously wicked. They scandalized Europe by their luxury, their avarice, their unblushing nepotism, and their crimes,"* analyzed one author. There was the "cupidity of Paul II, the cruelty of Sixtus IV, the unnatural passions of Alexander VI and the infidelities of Julius II." Machiavelli, not a Christian moralist, summed up the spiritual status of Italy, saying, "To the church and priests of Rome, we Italians owe this obligation—that we have become void of religion and corrupt." Like a John the Baptist, the voice of Savonarola began to sound out against the sins of the church, sparing no one, warning that the ax was to be laid at the root of the tree, calling men everywhere to repent!

As a youth, Savonarola had had no part in the paths of pleasure. He had lived a lonely life, agonizing over the world's lost condition, men's heedless rejection of Christ and His salvation, and the shame and corruption of the church. Under a sermon by an Augustinian friar, Savonarola's destiny was determined by a single word. Savonarola never revealed that word, but at the age of 23, he left home, entering a Dominican monastery at Bologna. For seven years he read and studied the Scriptures, until it was declared "he knew the Scriptures by heart from beginning to end."

In 1481, Savonarola was sent to Florence and the monastery of St. Mark's. Florence was the city of renown, the city of the Renaissance. Here Savonarola preached his first sermons, but they were rudely received. *"His rough accent, and his uncouth gestures displeased the fickle Florentines, who were much like the Athenians of old."*

At Brescia, Savonarola found his message. He had fasted, prayed and pored over the Bible, crying to God by day and night for a message from Heaven that would convert his people from their corrupt ways. In 1489 he returned to Florence and the Florentine revival was born.

One wrote of his message which shook Florence to its center:

> He wasted no time and he did not beat the air; he struck at the vices of Florence contrasting its outward culture with its hidden crime and sensuality. . .nor did he fail to lash out against the impurities of the church, or contrast its glaring immoralities with the splendor of its ceremonial and the sumptuousness of its ritual. At last in that land given over to licentiousness and crime, righteousness had found a voice. Here at last was a man of God, fearless, incorruptible. Here once more appeared the prophet, confronting the vicious of his day with unflinching courage, crying aloud. . ."Repent! Repent! For the day of vengeance is at hand."

His fearlessness, his fiery preaching and his unswerving faith brought him fame across the country. Crowds came, congregations swelled until he had to preach in the Cathedral. "Tears ran profusely, mourners beat upon their breasts, crying to God for mercy; the church echoed and re-echoed with their sobs."

Because of his unimpeachable character, his utter unselfishness and the power of his preaching, at the death

PROFILES IN EVANGELISM

of Lorenzo de Medici, the political power of Florence and the head of the house whose benefactions had bought off the clergy and the churchmen, Savonarola became the manager of the city, aye, its ruler. The city became a republic, the reforming preacher its governor, and the pulpit the seat of his power. For a season, Florence became a "New Jerusalem" to the point that, as one historian cited, *"the city on the days that Savonarola spoke had streets that were almost a desert. Houses, schools and shops were closed. No obscene songs were heard, but low or loud chants or lauds, psalms or spiritual songs. Vast sums were paid in restitution of old debts or wrongful gains. The dress of men became more sober, that of the women, modest and quiet."*

But righteousness and reformers for righteousness are not without enemies. Paramount among the enemies of Savonarola were factions within his Florence and the pope at Rome. The life of the reformer was a constant rebuke to the infamous life of Alexander VI and "licentious Rome could not exist with a regenerated Florence." To silence Savonarola, Alexander first used flattery, then bribes, actually offering Savonarola the office of cardinal and its hat. This aroused Savonarola to "intense indignation," and he insisted, "I will have no hat but that of a martyr, red in my own blood." It was a prophetic announcement, the following year "the glove was thrown aside, the mask put off, and the knife unsheathed" and a commission appointed by Alexander charged Savonarola with heresy.

It was inevitable. The masses which had once followed Savonarola as their master became fickle and faltered toward the pope, especially when he *"promised plenary indulgence to all who would renounce their new faith and return to the faith embodied in himself."* A feud between the Dominican order and Franciscan order erupted to the full and then orders came from Rome that Savonarola must die—"even if he be another John the Baptist."

May 22, 1498, he was condemned to die and the next day he was hanged, then burned. The bishop in charge of the execution condemned him: "I separate you from the church militant, and the church triumphant." *"Not from the church triumphant,"* spoke Savonarola with a loud voice, "that is beyond thy power."

Few men were ever more variously estimated than he. By one party he has been represented as an inspired prophet, a saint, a miracle worker; by another as ambitious, fanatical, even hypocritical. By one, a patriot; by another a demagogue. One writer wrote of him, *"Never before, perhaps, never since, have there been heard eloquence so sustained, earnestness so intense, passion for righteousness so concentrated, as were heard in those days, when from the pulpit in Duomo, Savonarola ruled Florence in the name of his Master, Jesus Christ."*

But another spoke it well and wisely when he wrote, of Savonarola, "Bearing himself with composure and fortitude, his last words were, 'O Florence, what hast thou done today?' "

"What indeed?" wrote Vedder. *"Nothing but postpone for four centuries Italy's deliverance from papal yoke."*

Lee R. Scarborough

Lee R. Scarborough

Evangelist

(1870-1945)

In a car recently, the name of Dr. Lee Scarborough was mentioned. My former pastor spoke out, *"I heard him only once, but he impressed me as being the most compassionate Christian I ever met."*

This appraisal of Dr. Cloyce Pugh was an articulate "Amen" to everything I have read about this pastor-evangelist-educator-author, who left as indelible an impact for soul winning upon America—especially in the ranks of Southern Baptists—as any other man in the first forty years of this Twentieth Century.

Dr. George Truett, notable Southern pastor and leader, likened Scarborough to the Apostle Paul:

> Ever since L. R. Scarborough found Christ precious to his soul as personal Saviour, his lofty spirit has been on fire for the salvation of the lost. . . .From the day of his definite, final decision to be a preacher, he has been one of the most prodigious workers in Christ's cause, of his own or any other generation. His ever-enlarging life has been Pauline, both in labors and in spirit.

Dr. Faris Whitesell, Moody Bible Institute, suggested the same when he wrote,

> When a student asked him the secret of his power, modestly he answered, "If I have any power, it is this: there is never an hour, day or night, but that I can close my eyes and weep over a lost world." This man stood in the same spiritual tradition with that other [Paul] who said, "I ceased not to warn every one night and day with tears" (Acts 20:31).

164   *PROFILES IN EVANGELISM*

Scarborough was born in Louisiana in 1870, in a Baptist minister's home, but was raised in West Texas, spending his youth as a cowboy. He dated his conversion at the age of 17, although he had joined a Baptist church two years before. A courthouse address by Judge K. K. Leggett, in Abilene, Texas, spurred the young Scarborough to get an education and begin the answer to his mother's prayer that he be called to preach the Gospel. He graduated from Baylor University and Yale. It was in Yale that he surrendered to preach, witnessing in his own words: "There is one period of three months in which I felt that call of God to preach and I fought it and rebelled against it; but, thank God, on the 16th day of April in 1896, in Old Farnum Hall at Yale University, in my room, on my bed, with a broken heart I yielded and I thank God that since that time I have been trying to do His will."

After that he attended Southern Baptist Theological Seminary in Louisville, Kentucky. After Louisville (1900) he pastored in Cameron, Texas, and Abilene, Texas. In 1908, he began a thirty-five-year association with Southwestern Baptist Theological Seminary, Fort Worth, Texas, as professor of evangelism—and for twenty-eight of those years as president of the institution. The chair of evangelism in those days of Scarborough was rightly called, "The Chariot of Fire!" Some of America's great living evangelists—*including Dr. John R. Rice and Dr. Hyman Appelman, etc.*—received some of their fire and force under the pungent, passionate, powerful lectures of Lee Scarborough. Would to God we had some "Scarboroughs" on "chariots of fire" in the classrooms of evangelism in our Bible colleges and seminaries today!

Scarborough was also an able author. His books excel in the field of evangelism. They are some of the most treasured titles I have in my library. Personal revival results in reading such books as *With Christ After the Lost,* a textbook on personal evangelism; *Endued to Win,* a treatise on evangelism in *Acts,* one of the richest books on this subject; *How Jesus Won Men;* etc. He also published sermon books on such subjects as, *The Tears of Jesus, Prepare to Meet God,* etc. The challenge to compassion, conquest for Christ, conversion to the lost cry out from almost every page and paragraph of this man's pen.

But, doubtlessly, as Dr. C. E. Matthews, superintendent of evangelism, Southern Baptist Convention, said: *"We believe that it was as a personal soul winner that he* [Scarborough] *stood out most prominently among preachers. In this field he was surely unsurpassed. He practiced soul winning almost constantly."*

In that, Scarborough practiced what he preached: "Every Christian is called in the hour of salvation to witness a winning testimony for Jesus Christ. Nothing in Heaven or earth can excuse him from it. God gives no furlough from the Heaven-born obligation."

Such persistent practice of personal evangelism occasioned this phrase from his pen: "I have won somebody to Christ every way Jesus did except up a tree and on a cross. And the first chance I get I am going after them. I think probably I won some where He didn't. I would not boast about it. I have tried to make it a habit to pick up men for Christ."

I wish space permitted a recitation of some of Lee Scarborough's soul-winning incidents. They would inspire, encourage, challenge and change us in our service for the Saviour, I am sure. But may I conclude this chapter with a quotation from this soul winner, sixteen years before his death.

> Oh, the joys and rich spiritual experiences of those who win souls. As I look back across the fifty-five years of my little life I remember a happy home, though it was in a log house, on the frontiers of Texas, the joy of a gloriously good father and mother, and remember the joys of my own happy home through now twenty-five years with my blessed companion and our six children. . . .As I look back over the years of study and recount the intellectual joys and the comradeships of my friends and remember the social joys, shining and rising above them all is the oft-repeated joy of my heart when I have been permitted by this same Saviour to bring to Him scarlet women,

infidels, atheists, gamblers, murderers, whoremongers, moralists, and all sorts, thousands and thousands of them. There is no joy like the joy of soul winning.

May every reader, along with this writer, pray this moment to God: *"Give me some of the same passion, purpose of life, power of the Spirit that possessed a Lee R. Scarborough."*

Gipsy Smith

Evangelist

(1860-1947)

Contrary to what is commonly believed by many Christians, Gipsy Smith was not converted to Christ as a sickly gypsy boy in a tent the first time he heard the Gospel by a missionary. Doubtlessly, this idea results from a wrong association with the hymn, "Tell It Again," which tenderly tells of a gypsy boy's conversion.

In his *Autobiography,* Smith, who was a real gypsy, tells how he was converted as a result of a number of crises experiences: the death of his mother and her doubtless deathbed repentance, the soon-following salvation of his father, his attendance at a Wesleyan chapel and the powerful convicting impact of that message, and his unfounded assumption that conversion occurs in families by age—the eldest to the youngest child. [*His three older brothers had been saved in that sequence and Smith was afraid his younger sister could not get saved until he did.*] The result was that this gypsy, born near Epping Forest, England, was saved at the age of sixteen, November 17, 1876.

A year later, the unschooled, unlettered gypsy left home to become an evangelist with the Salvation Army, where he served until 1882. Eighteen seventy-seven was an eventful year, for that same year he married one of his converts of Whitby, Miss Annie Pennock. Arming himself with a Bible and commentaries, the gypsy learned to read and to preach. He became one of the renowned evangelists of his generation, literally fulfilling the prayer of Ira Sankey, D.

Gipsy Smith

L. Moody's song leader, who once laid his hands upon the young gypsy and prayed, *"The Lord bless you and use you for His glory."*

His appearance, as a Lynn, Massachusetts, reporter penned it, was: "A short, wiry, thick-set gentleman, with an elastic, springy step, dressed in common, everyday suiting, without style. . .a head well rounded and finely formed, a face of fair finish, and clear countenance, brown as the berries of the autumn bush, a heavy, dark mustache; dark eyes that glisten like diamonds, with the zeal of religious enthusiasm; a magnificent head of hair, black as a raven's wing, and strikingly suggestive of the nomadic race that gave him birth."

Smith preached sharply against sin and was often salty, stinging in his speech. A woman said to him once: "I don't believe in revivals," to which the gypsy snapped back, "No, Madam; the Devil doesn't either." Yet his sermons were also saturated with a warmth of love and a wealth of homey truth. Smith preached the great truths. Deadly earnest in his presentation, he made no attempt to be funny. Added to his powerful and persuasive preaching (one author wrote: *"he knew how to persuade men"*) was his ministry of music. With his gypsy love of music and with a beautiful voice, Smith literally "sang sinners into Heaven." His services were informal; no stated order of a meeting was ever followed—*"I always say, I shall be stiff enough in my coffin."* And, *"I was born in a field, and you can't cram me into a flower pot."*

Smith's ministry was a success in England, where thousands thronged to hear him. Add Australia, too. And America—for the gypsy made countless voyages to preach and had to turn away crowds in many cities.

He also ministered to the troops in World War I. Some of his compassion for the crowd is seen in these heart-moving sentences:

> I was talking behind the lines to some of the boys. Every boy in front of me was going up to the trenches that night. There were five or six hundred of them.

PROFILES IN EVANGELISM

> It wasn't easy to talk. All I said was accompanied by the roar of guns, the crack of rifles, and the rattle of machine guns, and once in a while our faces were lit up by the flashes. I looked at those boys. I couldn't preach to them in any ordinary way. I knew, and they knew, that for many it was the last service for some on earth.
>
> I said, "Boys, you are going up to the trenches. Anything may happen there. I wish I could go with you. God knows I do. I would if they would let me, and if any of you fell, I would like to hold your hand and say something to you for your mother, for wife, and for lover, and for your little child. I'd like to be the link between you and home for just that moment—God's messenger for you. They won't let me go: but there is Somebody who will go with you. You know who that is." You should have heard the boys all over that hut whisper, "Yes, Sir, Jesus."
>
> "Well," I said, "I want every man that is anxious to take Jesus with him into the trenches to stand." Instantly and quietly every man stood.

Doubtless, this kind of a compassionate heart was the cardinal cause for Gipsy Smith's success everywhere in evangelism. He said so himself. After a meeting in Kansas City an old man came to him and put his hands on Smith's head. The gypsy described it further: "I bent forward in silence. I thought he was going to bless me. But instead of blessing me, he was feeling my head. "Are you a phrenologist?" I said. "No," he answered, "I am feeling for the secret of your success." "Well, my brother," I said, "you are too high. The secret of my success lies in my heart."

On August 4, 1947, Gipsy Smith died while en route to America, after seventy years of world-embracing evangelism that began when a gypsy boy, born in a tent, prayed, *"O God, I want to love Thee, I want to be saved, I want to be good, and I will follow Thee."*

Charles Haddon Spurgeon
The Pastor-Evangelist
(1834-1892)

Probably no preacher of all time ever more perfectly fulfilled the Bible injunction to pastors, ". . .do the work of an evangelist, make full proof of thy ministry" (II Tim. 4:5), than did Charles Haddon Spurgeon.

Spurgeon, who began preaching at the age of seventeen, built, under God, the Metropolitan Tabernacle of London, England, into the greatest soul-winning church and far-reaching pulpit the world has known since the apostolic church at Jerusalem.

Superlatives are the only words strong enough to speak of Spurgeon. Well was he called the "Prince of Preachers." No other man has ever been so worthy to wear his mantle.

Spurgeon was converted to Christ as a sin-smitten, heavy-hearted, fifteen-year-old boy after he heard a layman preacher cry out, *"Young man, you look very miserable. Young man, look to Jesus Christ. Look. Look. Look!"* Spurgeon heard and heeded the plea of the preacher. He realized for the first time it was "trusting and not trying!" And that wintry morning, December 15, 1850, Spurgeon was saved.

Two years later he was a pastor!—pastor of a little Baptist church at Waterbeach. And two years later he was called to pastor New Park Street Chapel. New Park was an historic church which had had such illustrious pastors as Benjamin Keach, John Gill and John Rippon. But when Spurgeon accepted the call—the congregation numbered

Charles Haddon Spurgeon

Charles Haddon Spurgeon 173

one hundred! And this in an auditorium that seated *one thousand and two hundred!*

In *three months* the church was crowded out. In less than a year it had to be enlarged. The day the new building was opened—it was too small! The congregation then built Metropolitan Tabernacle which seated five thousand and had standing room for another thousand. *For the next thirty-eight years Spurgeon filled the church and the standing area twice every Sunday!* As one biographer well wrote, "He never found but one place that could hold his congregation—the open fields roofed by skies!"

Prince of preachers indeed! As Dr. B. H. Carroll asked in his memorial address, February, 1892: "With whom among men can you compare him? He combined the preaching power of Jonathan Edwards and Whitefield with the organizing power of Wesley, and the energy of, fire and courage of Luther. In many respects he was most like Luther. In many, most like Paul."

Yes, measured by every human standard, Spurgeon was the prince of preachers. No other preacher ever commencing with such a large congregation commanded such increasing crowds until his death. No other preacher has ever had more messages published in the English language. Surely, no other preacher has had such a staggering total of sermons translated into foreign languages. The earth's greatest daily and weekly papers have carried his messages since the 1850's—over *one hundred years!* Of the publishing of books by this paragon of preachers there appears to be no end. Just a casual reference to some of his titles, is, at once, a catalogue of some of the most vital, valuable volumes that line a gospel preacher's library: *Treasury of David,* seven volumes on the Psalms, doubtlessly the richest reference written on the Psalms; *Lectures to Students,* two series; *Morning and Evening,* devotional readings; *Commenting on the Commentaries; Park Street Sermons; John Ploughman's Talks,* a volume of homespun, practical truths; *Sermon Notes on the Whole Bible,* four volumes; *Spurgeon*

174   *PROFILES IN EVANGELISM*

Memorial Library of Sermons; etc. His publications total about one hundred volumes, plus untold numbers of tracts, leaflets, papers, etc.

And he was an editor, too. In 1865, Spurgeon began publishing *The Sword and the Trowel,* a monthly magazine that preached salvation, crusaded for Christ, promoted revival and exposed modernism in the British Baptist Union.

But Spurgeon was more than pastor, author and editor. He was also an educator. In 1866, he founded the Pastor's College. Patterned after Samuel's school of the prophets, the college founded by faith by a twenty-two-year-old youth who had no college or theological school training himself, had no peer in its day. The evangelistic fervor, the spiritual power of Spurgeon filled and fired the students of his school to make an impact for revival and righteousness across Britain that is inestimable. One biographer related that "in one decade these students baptized twenty-six thousand, six hundred and seventy-six converted persons." May God give to our generation a Spurgeon, nay, many Spurgeons, and multiplied similar schools and multitudes of the same kind of students who will go forth to conquer for Christ in these desperate, deluded and destructive days!

Space prohibits more than mere mention of the Colportage society organized by Spurgeon. And to meet the social needs of society as well as the spiritual, Spurgeon started orphanages, widow's almshouses, etc.

Prince of preachers—beyond any denial or dispute. At fifty-seven years of age, after forty years of fullest, far-reaching, forever-enduring ministry, Charles Haddon Spurgeon, the pastor-evangelist, died in Mentone, France. Rightly did the speaker state from the Scriptures at the funeral: "Know ye not that there is a prince and a great man fallen this day in Israel?" (II Sam. 3:38).

Billy Sunday

Giant for God Among Evangelists

(1863-1935)

Contemporary evangelism will probably never again see the equal of William Ashley Sunday, better known as "Billy" Sunday. Adjectives are hardly adequate vehicles to describe this former big league ball player who was a curbstone recruit to Christ.

Sunday's conversion, like his life, was sensational and spectacular. Seated one Sunday afternoon, "tanked up" on a curb in Chicago, Sunday listened with keen interest to a Salvation Army gospel team, accepted their invitation to attend the Pacific Garden Mission that night, and was saved!

Converted to Christ, and captivated by Christ, Sunday soon quit the ball diamond for Christian work, leaving a $500-a-month contract for a $83.33 a month salary with the YMCA. Sunday later became an associate of Evangelist J. Wilbur Chapman; and in 1896, at the age of thirty-four, Billy Sunday entered full-time evangelism.

It would take multiplied more space than this volume allows to describe one of God's greatest soul-winning evangelists, called by his associate, Dr. Homer Rodeheaver, "the greatest gospel preacher since Paul" and considered by others to be the "most spectacular evangelist since John the Baptist." What words weigh enough to measure this man and his ministry whose crusades caused more than a million people to "hit the sawdust trail" for salvation; crusades that caused righteousness to be restored in countless wicked cities, cleaned up lives, homes, closed

Billy Sunday

Billy Sunday   *177*

down movies, saloons and bawdy houses like no evangelist had ever done before and as no one has done *since!*

"*Colorful*" must be one word, for Sunday's preaching was not the stilted, stentorian sermons of the "clergyman," but "words that smack of the street, the shop," denunciatory, excoriating, sizzling, blistering vocabulary against sin and hypocrisy:

> I'm no spiritual masseur or osteopath. I'm a surgeon, and I cut deep.
> They tell me a revival is only temporary. So is a bath, but it does you good.
> It won't save your soul if your wife is a Christian. You've got to be something more than a brother-in-law to the church.
> They say to me, "Bill, you rub the fur the wrong way." I don't; let the cats turn 'round.

"*Sensational*" must be another description of Sunday. He was at once in his preaching an actor, an acrobat and an athlete. As an actor, Sunday made scenes and people live. He was Naaman, the leper, sticking his big toe in the river and stubbing it against a big rock, screaming out, "O-o-o-o-o!" As an acrobat he raced back and forth across the platform (one editor estimated Sunday traveled a mile in every message). Sunday broke chairs, stood on the pulpit, jumped from the platform into the pews to preach to one man to be saved. As an athlete he slid across the platform face first, depicting a former ball-playing friend getting called "out" at Heaven by God, the Umpire. One of my Sunday school superintendents told me Sunday's message, "You're Out," was the most vivid message he had ever heard.

The sermon subject, "You're Out," leads me to suggest some of the other captivating, compelling subjects Sunday preached: "Some Nuts for Skeptics to Crack," "Chickens Come Home to Roost," "Hot Cakes Off the Griddle," "The Devil's Boomerang." It was that last sermon to which Homer Rodeheaver, Sunday's associate for many years, witnessed:

> Until he tempered it down a little, (it) had one ten-

178 *PROFILES IN EVANGELISM*

minute period in it where two to twelve men fainted every time I heard him preach it. But, as a result, thousands of men went home with lives dedicated to God and purity for the sake of future health of wives and babies.

"Novel" is another word that must be used. Sunday was not the first evangelist to organize his campaigns into great spiritual crusades; but nobody ever did it on a bigger, grander scale before, and probably no one has ever done it any better. The great "Sunday" tabernacles built to seat 20,000, the "sawdust trail," the delegations, the follow-up program, the great music and choirs, the parades, the cottage prayer meetings, are all part of a great legacy Sunday left evangelism.

But if one does not say of Billy Sunday's ministry that it was *"supernatural,"* he has seen only the sensational in Sunday and not the spiritual! For Sunday's successes lay not in his colorful language, nor his acrobatic, energetic style, nor his organizational genius. Sunday's success was born of these supreme spiritual qualities:

(1) "Unreserved consecration to the task of preaching the Gospel, born of an unswerving faith in the infallibility of the Scripture and belief in God's plan of salvation."*

(2) A consummate conviction of the lostness of sinners and a Christ-begotten compassion to win them to the Saviour.

(3) A passionate, importunate prayer-life.

(4) The awareness of the anointing of the Holy Spirit on his ministry and his absolute need of the Spirit's empowering. Invariably he opened the Bible and placed his sermon notes upon the passage in Isaiah— first verse of the sixty-first chapter—which reads, "The Spirit of the Lord God is upon me; because the Lord hath anointed me to preach good tidings. . . ."

Billy Sunday has been dead for over 30 years now, dying at the age of 72. A new generation of youth and children have come upon the scene who have never heard of him. We

Billy Sunday 179

find ourselves in a day of "easy-come, easy-go" evangelism, and a day of ecumenical evangelism. I find myself praying as I pen these words, *"God make me, and make our evangelists, pastors and members, people who will pray the same prayer and pay the same price William Ashley Sunday did when he cried to God, 'I WANT TO BE A GIANT FOR GOD!'"*

* From book, *20 Years With Billy Sunday*, by Homer Rodeheaver. Used by permission of the Rodeheaver Co.

T. DeWitt Talmage

T. DeWitt Talmage
Evangelistic Pastor
(1832-1902)

If Charles Haddon Spurgeon was the "Prince of Preachers," T. DeWitt Talmage must be considered as one of the princes of the American pulpit. In fact, Spurgeon stated of Talmage's ministry: "His sermons take hold of my inmost soul. The Lord is with this mighty man. I am astonished when God blesses me, but not surprised when He blesses him."

And, like Spurgeon, Talmage's ministry was multiplied not only from the pulpit to immense congregations, but in the printed pages of newspapers and in the making of many books. For thirty-nine years, without exception of a week, through the syndicates in 3,600 newspapers, Talmage's sermons spoke to an estimated thirty million readers weekly in America and in translations in most European nations and many Asiatic countries. Over fifty volumes of his books were circulated across the country, also.

And for twenty-five years Talmage filled the four-to-five-thousand-seat auditorium of his Brooklyn church, as well as auditoriums across America and the British Isles. He counted converts to Christ in the thousands annually, attesting that one year six thousand confessed Christ.

Frederick Frelinghausen figured Talmage's sermons as "unequalled in their power to commend Christ to men as a never-dying Saviour," and Dr. Prime praised the man's messages as being "as simple as Bunyan's, as cogent as Wesley's and as mighty as Edwards'."

PROFILES IN EVANGELISM

Yes, it is safe to say, T. DeWitt Talmage was some preacher—aye, a prince of American pulpits!

Yet the president of New Brunswick Theological Seminary had his doubts as to whether the young student Talmage would ever make a preacher, let alone a prince of preachers. After the seminarian's first sermon, his president told Talmage tersely, ". . .*frankly, and in all kindness, I must tell you that I solemnly think you have made a mistake in your calling. Get a position selling goods behind a dry goods counter or take a clerkship in a law office, or, if necessary, follow the plow, but do not think of becoming pastor of a church. You are not fitted for it at all. It is a great mistake for you to waste your time.*"

Fortunately, Talmage did not follow DeWitt's counsel and protested that he would go on and graduate. And he did. And Talmage preached "to his hundreds where the venerable president DeWitt preached to his one," once again proving another college and seminary president wrong about a "preacher-boy."

Talmage took his first church, a Reformed church at Belleville, New Jersey, immediately after graduation. He had been raised in a devout Dutch family with a strong Christian influence, but did not become a Christian himself until he was eighteen years of age. Six years after his conversion he was a pastor. From his Belleville pastorate, Talmage took similar churches in Syracuse and Philadelphia, and then after thirteen years among the Reformed people, Talmage took the pastorate of the Central Presbyterian Church of Brooklyn, New York.

As Dr. Charles Banks wrote in a biography of Talmage, ". . .*with Dr. Talmage's life work will Brooklyn always be associated. There he found his real field—the field which as thoroughly fitted him as he it. . . .*"

At the time Talmage had calls from prosperous congregations in Chicago and San Francisco, but he took the nearly impoverished pastorate in Brooklyn which had nineteen voting members and could only promise him, "they would do what they could," and that he could have a "free church" (no pew rental).

Soon the pastor and people began to build the Free Tabernacle, a horseshoe-shaped building that enclosed nearly one half an acre in area. Every one of the fifteen hundred seats were to be free—no rental, nor dues to be levied, a radically new innovation in that day. The building was dedicated September 25, 1870. Two years and three months later (December 22, 1872) it burned to the ground. The congregation built another one, this time to seat over four thousand. Unbelievably, on another Sunday morning, October 27, 1889, it burned. And incredibly, the third tabernacle burned down on a Sunday morning, May 13, 1894.

Although Dr. Talmage interpreted these fires as "blessings in disguise," the third fire proved to be the crowning blow to the trials of the Tabernacle congregation and ultimately led to his resignation and his acceptance of a pastorate in Washington, D. C.

But what a twenty-five years' ministry it was! Talmage had pastored the "largest Protestant church in the entire world," had founded the Tabernacle Lay College, had edited the *Christian Herald* and other religious periodicals.

In 1899, Talmage resigned the Washington pulpit to devote his entire time to preaching, writing and lecturing. Since 1860 he had been a world-renowned lecturer as well as preacher. And, as an author, Talmage wrote some notable volumes, one, *From the Manger to the Throne*, the life of Christ written on a trip to the Holy Land in 1889.

One has only to read his writings to realize something of the man's understanding of the human heart and its needs. His messages were scholarly, but simple, eloquent but earnest and evangelistic, and were often considered sensational in his day. (Talmage was tried by his synod for "buffoonery in the pulpit" and accused of "being an actor doing sensational things for the sake of attention." But Talmage testified he took Christ for his model and that his illustrations were "commonplace like Christ's.") It is

184 PROFILES IN EVANGELISM

evident that, like in Christ's ministry, "the common people heard him gladly."

On April 12, 1902, Talmage passed on—undeniably a prince of preachers "whose sermons Queen Victoria included among her favorite books," and a preacher whose personal friendship was highly valued by the Czar of Russia, and the preacher to multiplied millions of the English and non-English speaking world from his pulpit—the weekly newspaper pages.

J. Hudson Taylor

Pioneer Missionary

(1832-1905)

"He must move men through God—by prayer," that was the philosophy of J. Hudson Taylor, first missionary to the interior of China and the founder of the China Inland Mission. And from that December day when as a teenager he heard from Heaven, "Go for Me to China," this young Englishman set out to prove his philosophy. That he did so successfully and miraculously makes for some of the most exciting reading in the records of evangelism.

After his call Taylor first moved from the comforts of his home with his parents and two sisters in beautiful Barnsley of Yorkshire to Drainside, Hull, a poverty-stricken, depressing area named after and notorized by its foul ditch. Taylor had gone there purposely to work for a doctor and accumulate a little medical knowledge, and also to accustom himself to something of the loneliness and dangers of living in a strange land where his only companion would be God.

It was at Drainside Taylor learned one can trust God with his last cent. He had been called out late one night to witness to and pray over a sick woman with starving children. As he tried to pray, his words choked in his mouth because he had in his possession a silver coin that would answer his prayer and alleviate their sufferings somewhat. "Hypocrite!" he heard his heart condemn him. "Telling people about a kind and loving Father in Heaven—*and not prepared to trust Him yourself,* without your money!" He gave them his last coin—only one bowl of porridge between

J. Hudson Taylor

him and poverty! As he ate that last meal he remembered the Scripture, "He that giveth to the poor lendeth to the Lord."

The next day he received a package. In it was a gold coin—worth ten times the silver coin. Taylor cried out triumphantly, "That's good interest! Ha! Ha! Invested in God's bank for twelve hours and it brings me this! That's the bank for me!"

Thus at nineteen years of age, Taylor learned he could trust and obey God in every area of his life. There were many lessons to learn, but at the first he learned that a man can take God at His Word. Three years earlier he had taken Christ and trusted Him as his Saviour. At sixteen years of age Taylor had already been disappointed and sated with life. He found the religious life of his parents very dull, although he attended church very dutifully with them. He really desired horses, hunting, luxuries. Alone at home one day he looked for something to read. He picked up a gospel tract and began to read it. At the very same moment seventy miles away his mother was earnestly praying for her son's salvation. That same day Taylor prayed—his first prayer—and it was answered. He was converted to Christ!

Praying! And answers to prayer! That became the passion of his life. He learned to move men through God by prayer. He asked no man for any material thing. He laid all needs before his Lord. That doctor he had worked for at Drainside had suggested to his young assistant, "Taylor, please do remind me when it is time to pay your salary. I'm so busy, you know, I'm quite likely to forget." And forget he did. But Taylor remembered that in China he would have no one to ask anything of, only God, so he simply asked God to remind the doctor.

Three weeks later the doctor remembered—but only after he had banked his money. Taylor was broke. It was Saturday. He had no money to pay his rent. He had no money for food. He prayed as he worked until ten o'clock, glad he would not have to face his landlady. As he prepared

188   *PROFILES IN EVANGELISM*

to leave, the doctor surprised him, "What do you think? One of my patients has just come to pay his bill! He's one of my richest patients and he could have paid me by check anytime. Yet, here he is, bringing in the money at ten o'clock on Saturday night." Then he added, "By the way, Taylor, you might as well take these notes. I have no change, but I can give you the balance of your salary next week. . .Good night."

Taylor's prayers were answered. He could not only pay his rent, he had money in hand for weeks ahead—but more than that, he had proven again: *God answers prayer and moves men.* He could go on to China!

And he did! There were storms at sea and miraculous deliverances in that five-and-one-half *months'* journey to China. There was civil war when he landed at Shanghai, rebels holding the city. Fires, famine, fearsome circumstances were fought by the young missionary on his knees and God delivered him. And at the age of twenty-two, eight months a missionary, he also found himself responsible for supplying the needs of newly-arriving missionaries, the Parker family.

Taylor ministered in the river towns, married a wife and saw many miracles in converted Chinese. But on June 25, 1865, he made his move to minister to the millions of China "West of the Mountains, South of the Clouds, North of the Lake"— Inland China. At Brighton, England, on furlough, he opened a bank account: "Ten pounds" (Fifty dollars) in the name of "The China Inland Mission." His initial goal was twenty-four workers. The next May the twenty-four sailed. Then there were seventy more. And another hundred. And finally more than eight hundred missionaries ministered across the far-flung miles of China's interior. Truly this man of faith and fortitude had mastered in the ministry of moving men through God by prayer.

J. Hudson Taylor died in 1905, before the communist takeover of his beloved China. His days were days of extensive and effective evangelism. Multitudes of converted

Chinese will rise up in Heaven and call him blessed. And many Christian workers whose lives were challenged and changed by the contagious Christian character of Taylor will follow in their train.

Reuben Archer Torrey

Reuben Archer Torrey

Evangelist

(1856-1928)

How many godly mothers there have been behind the God-used, God-honored giants of the Gospel, only God's records will reveal in eternity. But count R. A. Torrey's mother in that glorious group. For when that brilliant young collegian ran away from his home because of his falling into infidelity and utter unbelief, he could not and he did not run away from his mother's prayers and her pressing plea to Torrey the day he left home: *"My son, if you ever come to the darkest day in your life, as you will, you remember the only way is your mother's God."*

Torrey came to that day. Despaired of living, in the depths of the darkness of infidelity, Torrey decided to take his life, but, "the Spirit of God flashed through his mind what his mother had said, and he fell upon his knees and looked into the face of his mother's God, saw Calvary and he was born again."

Immediately after his conversion, Torrey set out to win souls to his Saviour. It was to be the pattern and the paramount practice of his life. Torrey's first convert was the young lady whom he had been taking to dances. "The first time I saw her after my conversion, I commenced to reason with her out of the Scriptures. It took two hours of talking to her, but she accepted Christ," Torrey told of his first soul-winning effort.

"Reasoning" was the right word when it came to Reuben Torrey. "Possessed with a brilliant, well-trained mind, he was logical, penetrating, positive, thorough and

192   PROFILES IN EVANGELISM

convincing, whether preaching, teaching or doing personal work." And Torrey practiced all three. He became a Congregational pastor in Garrettsville, Ohio; then a superintendent of city missions in Minneapolis; then superintendent of Moody Bible Institute and pastor of the Moody Church; and then pastor of the Church of the Open Door in Los Angeles and dean of the Bible Institute of Los Angeles.

It was because of his outstanding scholastic ability and evangelistic fervor that D. L. Moody hand-picked Torrey to become the superintendent of his infant Bible Institute, a position Torrey held from 1889 to 1908. Torrey laid the foundation "upon which the great work of the school's latter years was accomplished." He instituted the existing curriculum and practical Christian work program, organized the extension department in 1897, the correspondence school in 1901, and laid the groundwork for the evening school which began in 1903. It will always and rightly be known as "Moody's school," but the impact, the influence and the imprint of Reuben Torrey is still very much in evidence in Moody Bible Institute.

In 1921, Torrey became dean of Biola, where he served until 1924, pastoring the Church of the Open Door from 1915 to 1924, also.

And Torrey was an evangelist—one of America's greatest. Frequently he took extended periods of time to engage in campaigns in major American cities, as well as around the world. The greatest spiritual awakening Australia has ever experienced was during a Torrey campaign.

Although he was recognized as a great brain, Torrey's ministry was marked by *simplicity*. The befuddled, booze-brained skid-row men could understand his preaching. And his ministry was marked by *authority*. Torrey believed and preached *the Book!* "He believed the Holy Spirit would take the Word as His sword and cut through the darkness of the unbelieving mind, bringing light and conversion." And He did! Hosts of skeptics, infidels and atheists were saved under Torrey's ministry. In fact, Torrey had a singular success with that crowd. Robert Harkness, for many years Torrey's pianist, wrote of him: *"He was skilled in the art of meeting the difficulties of the unbeliever. He was powerful in answering the hackneyed arguments of the infidel."*

And Torrey was an author, able and authoritative. His *How to Work for Christ,* 518 pages, which contains the first real textbook on personal work, "How to Bring Men to Christ"; and "Ten Reasons Why the Bible Is the Word of God," are considered classics. And he penned many other books of sermons and Bible studies.

But like many another giant for God, Torrey shone best, furthest and brightest as a personal soul winner. "His highest ambition was to win souls." Speaking in the South London Tabernacle Torrey said, "I would rather win souls than be the greatest king or emperor on earth; I would rather win souls than be the greatest poet, or novelist, or literary man who ever walked the earth. My one ambition in life is to win as many as possible. Oh, it is the only thing worth doing, to save souls; and men, and women, we can all do it!" Amen and Amen!

Mel Trotter

Mel Trotter

Skid-Row Slave to Skid-Row Mission Superintendent

(1870-1940)

January 19, 1897, was another date in the calendar of Heaven when the saving grace of God reached down again to redeem, revitalize and restore a drunken sot—this time one so sated of his sin, so shackled in his sin that he was determined to commit suicide that very night by jumping into Lake Michigan!

The man that night was Mel Trotter, such a slave to his sin that he would sell his baby's shoes to get some money to buy another shot of liquor to try to satisfy his unslaked thirst for booze—and who shortly before had made a solemn oath before his wife and God over that dead baby's body that he would never touch another drop; a vow that was violated before the baby's burial!

The place of that memorable conversion was Pacific Garden Mission, Chicago, the scene of countless other conversions of similar souls who had been deceived, duped, doomed and become decrepit by the Devil's drink. On his way that night to Lake Michigan, Mel staggered into the mission, so drunken the doorman had to prop him up against a wall so he would not fall off the chair. Harry Monroe, a converted counterfeiter, was leading the music. As he led the song service, he prayed for that hulk of human hopelessness: *"O God, save that poor, poor boy."* At the conclusion of the service he gave the invitation, ending his appeal: "Jesus loves you, and so do I." Trotter raised

PROFILES IN EVANGELISM

his hand for prayer, jumped to his feet and came forward. And Harry Monroe led Mel Trotter to Christ. Thus began another articulate amen to the truth of II Corinthians 5:17, *"Therefore if any man be in Christ, he is a new creature: old things are passed away; behold, all things are become new."*

For the next two years Trotter never even read a newspaper, but saturated his mind and soul from his two-and-one-half-cent New Testament. In his new-found joy of salvation he told practically everyone he met about Jesus. Trotter got a job in a barber shop but spent every evening in the Mission. He could play the guitar a little, and also could sing, so he and Monroe sang duets, testified, and often went into churches to represent the Mission.

Three years after his conversion, Trotter, along with Monroe and some others, went to Grand Rapids, Michigan, at the invitation of a group of businessmen interested in a rescue mission in that city. The result of those conferences was a rescue mission, $1,100 raised to commence it, and to everyone's surprise, Mel Trotter was chosen superintendent, "although he had never led a mission meeting in his life."

The Mission opened. The crowds came. Souls were saved, lives transformed, families reunited. Of course, not without incident! Every night in those early days some group tried to break up the meeting with loud talking, laughing, singing dirty words to the songs, and often physical violence and villainy. Trotter introduced what was called "muscular Christianity" which he applied himself as, when one night, "Big Jack," one of Grand Rapid's most notorious barroom fighters, was gotten drunk and brought to the Mission to break up the meeting. A witness wrote later: *"I think if I had been at the door right then, I would never have let him in, but, no doubt it was the best thing that ever could happen, because when it was over, the 'Ole Man' (Trotter) was a little the worse for wear, but we needed an ambulance for Jack. I never saw a man so well whipped."* About two days later Jack came down to the Mission, gave himself to the Lord, and became one of the workers there.

But basically the Mission was run by love rather than force. Trotter, who had been saved by the recreative power of God from a life of debauchery and despair, "knew the needs of human hearts, whether they were hungry or self-satisfied, proud or stricken, broken and despairing," and he had the heart to help them.

The Mission on Lower Monroe Street grew and "naturally converts spread out through all the state and beyond." Soon other cities sensed the need and asked for a mission. First, it was Saginaw; then Muskegon; then Kalamazoo; then Milwaukee; South Bend; Los Angeles; Holland, Michigan; Dayton; Memphis and Omaha. Forty years later there were sixty-eight missions!

Trotter's ministry extended even further than his vast chain of branch missions. Although he considered himself strictly a mission man," he did evangelistic work around the world. He assisted Dr. Torrey in Toronto, speaking in the overflow meetings and often winning more converts there than Torrey did in Massee Hall. He regularly spoke for Billy Sunday on the last Monday of his campaigns and when the "Sawdust Evangelist" was ill or had to be absent. In World War I years, Trotter entered YMCA work and preached in fifty-four camps in twenty months, seeing 15,000 of the troops profess Christ.

"There is no question in my mind, that the greatest day I ever lived was the 19th of January, 1897, when the Lord Jesus came into my life and saved me from sin. That transaction revolutionized my entire life. It included my mind, my body and my soul," Trotter testified. Then he would charge: "Don't call me a reformed drunkard. I am a transformed man, a child of God."

Aye, that he was. He was a living testimonial for forty-three years of the truth of his favorite text, II Corinthians 5:17, for he rose from the depths of depravity of sin at twenty-three years of age to become the superintendent of Pacific Garden Mission, along with the one in Grand

PROFILES IN EVANGELISM

Rapids, the founder of sixty-eight others, and a soul winner that left a trail of converts to Christ that stretched around the world when he died at the age of seventy.

Yes, ". . .if any man be in Christ, he is a new creature; old things are passed away; behold, all things are become new."

"And what God has done for others—He can do for you."

Dr. George W. Truett

Pastor-Evangelist

(1867-1944)

When the names of America's truly great preachers are mentioned, the name of George Truett is almost always included. I have met men who have heard him herald the Gospel and everyone, without exception, acclaimed him to be one of the peers of all preachers they had been privileged to hear.

Recently, while in Dallas, Texas, I had opportunity to tour the historic First Baptist Church, which for years has been one of the largest Baptist churches in membership and stewardship in the Southern Baptist Convention—aye, in the nation and the world. George Truett was pastor of that colossus among churches for forty-seven years, bringing it from a standard-sized church building until it occupied a city block in downtown Dallas.

North Carolina was Truett's birthplace—Blue Ridge mountain country, Haysville, in Clay County. It was there he was converted to Christ and joined the church. He had been deeply concerned about his soul earlier, particularly at age eleven, but it was not until he returned home from teaching in a one-roomed schoolhouse at Crooked Creek, across the line in Georgia, that Truett was saved.

It was in Hiawassee, Georgia, where Truett was tutoring mountain children and when he was twenty-two years old, that an incident occurred which was to influence the rest of his life! Dr. John E. White witnessed of the incident thusly: "The Georgia Baptist Convention was in session. Fred C. McConnell. . .was down from the mountains in Rabun

George W. Truett

County with the story of the struggle for the mountain boys and girls of Hiawassee." To prove a point of the potential of the school and the students he called for Truett. He did not immediately appear. When he was found, "the pale, twenty-two-year-old mountain youth was forced out into the aisle of the courthouse and vastly embarrassed by the focus of eyes. 'Brethren, this is George Truett and he can speak like Spurgeon. George, tell them what the Lord has done for you and what you are trying to do up in the mountains.' "

Truett told. Great Georgia men were moved and melted by his simple, but powerful, pleading appeal for a college education for his students—something that had been denied him. Calder B. Willingham, of Macon, rose to his feet and said, "I want the honor of giving that young man a college education. If he will come to Macon I will pay his expenses at Mercer University until he graduates."

But, incredibly enough, Truett never attended Mercer. He went to Texas. His father had purposed to move to the Lone Star State and George Truett, twenty-two years old, obediently went with him. But he went to college—Baylor University—although not as a student. He was offered the position of financial secretary and was instrumental in saving Baylor from bankruptcy. Afterward he became a student, graduated, and unbelievably was elected to become Baylor's president! But already a pastor at East Waco Baptist Church, the then thirty-year-old Truett declined, stating that "God had given him the shepherd heart, and he could not entertain the thought of leaving the pastorate."

Married and a minister, Truett's plans were to devote his life to that pleasant church and city, but the same year of his graduation, he was called to the First Baptist Church of Dallas. The Lord's leading was definitely to Dallas and in September, 1897, the Truett's entered that ministry which would only be terminated by his death in 1944.

When Truett turned down the presidency of Baylor because God had given him a shepherd heart, he probably put his finger on the one attribute and ability from Heaven that marked him a man among and above many men—for many are the writers and biographers who explain his genius with the phrase "heart power." Truett had a heart for the city, the country, the cultured, the common, aye, even the cowboys. I have met men who heard Truett minister at cowboy camp meetings, where out-on-the-range men of the saddle would sit and thrill to the charm and clarity of Truett as he preached the Gospel of Christ. Many a careless and corrupt living cowpoke was convicted and hit the trail to start "ridin' " for Christ.

He had many pulpits besides the pulpit at First Baptist Church. He instituted the Palace Theater services in Dallas, held each noon the week before Easter. Nearly two thousand attended those services now in their 53rd year. He preached out in the country churches all across the South, and the common folk heard him gladly. And he preached from the steps of the nation's Capitol, and in world centers of London, Stockholm, Paris, Berlin, Jerusalem etc. And everywhere Truett's preaching produced souls for Christ.

He being dead yet speaketh! In my library I have six of his books of sermons. Though they are simply reductions of his messages to manuscript form, there is an eloquence and an evangelistic spirit on every page. They are Scripture-saturated, Saviour-extolling, heart-to-heart communicating. I get a revival of purpose and passion to seek souls and serve the Saviour better each time I read them.

I think Truett's biographers knew whereof they spoke when they explained the man and his ministry in these two well-defined words: *"heart power."*

"Uncle John" Vassar

Apostle of Personal Evangelism

(1813-1878)

The story is hoary-headed with age, but it is as true a tribute as ever was told of Uncle John Vassar:

While waiting in the parlor. . .he opened conversation with a very fashionable and proud-looking lady who was sitting in the room. With great concern he began to urge the necessity of the new birth and immediate acceptance of Christ upon her. She was thunderstruck, and protested that she did not believe in any of those things. Then followed a most fervent appeal, texts of Scripture, warnings against rejecting Christ, the certainty of wrath to come. . .Suddenly the gentleman came in for whom Vassar was waiting and called him out. In a moment the lady's husband came in.

"There has been an old man here talking to me about religion," she said.

"Why did you not shut him up?" he asked gruffly.

"He is one of those persons you can't shut up," was her reply.

"Why did you not tell him to mind his own business, then?" the lady's husband suggested.

"IF YOU HAD SEEN HIM YOU WOULD HAVE THOUGHT HE WAS ABOUT HIS BUSINESS," was her answer.

Aye, soul winning was the one, the only, the always-at-it business of John Vassar. For thirty-seven years after his conversion to Christ, this former Poughkeepsie, New York, brewery worker *"lived but for a single end, the glory of God, and the salvation of souls."* That is not just an eloquent,

PROFILES IN EVANGELISM

elegant eulogy. Excerpts from his diary and biographies emphasize the truth:

> I visit frequently forty families a day, have a meeting somewhere every night, and speak to three Sunday schools where practical every Lord's Day. I have counseled with over three thousand people during the last three months on the subject of personal religion. . . . I have visited the nineteen towns of this county, and some of them twice over. I have walked on an average of twenty miles a day, and spoken publicly about every night. I believe some good has been done, but I take to myself no praise.

Rev. J. Hyatt Smith told this tale of a stormy night: "He [Vassar] surprised me by coming at my house. I urged him to remain awhile. He refused and left that night on a steamer for Detroit. The boat was so crowded that I was afraid to have him go on board. I remember his look as he replied, 'I rejoice that so many are going. I shall have a blessed time working for souls!' "

Aye, souls were his business. During the Civil War, Vassar went to be with the Federal troops. He refused the chaplaincy at one hundred and twenty-five dollars a month to remain as colporteur for the American Tract Society at a wage of twenty-five dollars a month. *"He began his day at roll-call, and was in a state of intense activity from sixteen to eighteen hours a day. He ate little and slept little. . . . To very few of the eight thousand officers and men of that division in the time he was with them, he did not talk, and to the majority of them more than once or twice. . . . Conversing with from seventy-five to one hundred men a day, he came to fiftieth or sixtieth just as fresh in his manner, just as interesting, just as tender, as at the first."*

His seeking souls was nationwide. "He traveled from Maine to Florida, from the Atlantic Coast to the Pacific, on foot, on horseback, by rail, by steamer. . .in one intense, eager pursuit of souls. . . ." Army camps, freed men and poor whites in the South; miners in Colorado, Nevada, California; the Mormons in Utah; settlers in the plains of Kansas; hardy mountaineers in Kentucky and Tennessee;

as well as staid New Englanders, all heard and felt the impact of the powerful praying, exhorting and personal pleading of Uncle John Vassar for them to "be born again."

> Every man he met he sought opportunity to enquire of his spiritual state, and if he were not a Christian, he warned him in the name of Christ, and with tears of the deceit and danger of sin and entreated him to forsake sin and to turn to God.
>
> When he called on President Grant, after he paid him the respect due the chief Executive of the United States, he held on to his hand until he had told him of the Lord Jesus Christ, and courteously questioned him regarding his experience of the new birth. Introduced to Brigham Young, the Mormon leader, he made the same appeal and pressed the same searching question concerning his soul.

In 1878, Vassar died at the age of sixty-five, literally burned out for his Lord. Dr. Stevenson, secretary of the Tract Society, called him *"the most laborious and most useful Christian layman of his day."* Vassar refused ordination, striving only to help pastors in soul winning. He called himself "the Good Shepherd's dog, hunting up lost sheep." Dr. S. H. Tyng, Jr., called him "the dear old *soul-trap.*" H. V. Miller, one of his biographers, called him the "Apostle of Personal Evangelism." His friends affectionately called him "Uncle John." But to thousands upon thousands in eternity, he will be *"the man who led me to the Lord."*

Reading his biographies, one is impressed with some crowning characteristics of Vassar—characteristics that must possess us if we will succeed in soul winning: He was *a man of prayer*—"almost unbroken intercourse with God in prayer. He absolutely prayed day and night. Prayed about everything. Prayed for almost everybody. . . ." *"He was a mighty man of faith."* "He possessed a remarkable *persistency of purpose."* "Unflinching *loyalty to Christ."* "Deep and tender *sympathy."* "Saw a soul to be saved, and realized its worth." "Intimate and thorough knowledge of the Bible."

Faris Whitesell, in his Moody Pocket Book, *Great*

Personal Workers, wrote these wise words. May they warn and warm us:

Is not the greatest need of the Christian world today for men of Uncle John Vassar's all-out dedication to personal soul winning? No one could be exactly like Uncle John, nor would God wish him to be; but if his Christian character, self-sacrifice and burning zeal for the salvation of the lost could be matched in even one hundred men and women of our day, would not the revival we desire be upon us in a short time?

John Wesley

Evangelist

(1703-1791)

When some Epworth, England, villagers, on February 9, 1709, formed a human ladder and pulled a five-and-one-half-year-old boy named John Wesley through the second-story window of a burning parsonage, these rescuers plucked as a "brand from the fire" one who, under God, would be largely responsible for saving England from the blood bath of a French revolution by building the fires of the great Wesleyan revival!

The night John Wesley was saved from his blazing bedroom, England was at its lowest depths of depravity: morally, spiritually and politically. J. Wesley Bready described that day thusly:

> . . .Stark skepticism gripped the lives of the leaders in religion and government. The church prelates were blind guides. The court life was unchaste and indecent. The sinful social life fostered horrible conditions for children, universal gambling, and such unchristian practices as slavery, unspeakable prison condition, political bribery and corruption. Ghastly drunkenness and vicious sensuality were the accepted order.

England was ripe for either *"a visitation of the judgment of God or an outpouring of the Spirit of God in revival power."* The Wesleyan revival brought the blessings of the latter!

Wesley was the fifteenth of nineteen children born to Samuel Wesley, a Church of England minister. Although raised in a parsonage, under the preaching of his father and the prayers of his mother, Susannah, John Wesley was not

John Wesley

John Wesley

saved until after he had served a term as missionary to the Indians in the American colony of Georgia. In his *Journal*, under the date of January 24, 1738, we read the hollowness and hopelessness of his hungry soul: "I went to America to convert the Indians, but, oh, who shall convert me? Who, what is he that shall deliver me from this evil heart?"

But Wesley became converted! The debasing failures of his ministry in Georgia, the faithful spiritual counsel and example of the Moravian missionaries—particularly Peter Bohler—and his ceaseless searching the Scriptures for light and life led to his well-known Aldersgate experience, May 24, 1738. Wesley wrote of his conversion in his *Journal*:

> In the evening, I went very unwillingly to a society in Aldersgate Street, where one was reading LUTHER'S PREFACE TO THE EPISTLE OF ROMANS. About a quarter before nine, while he was describing the change which God works in the heart through faith in Christ, I felt my heart strangely warmed. . . .
>
> I felt I did trust in Christ, Christ alone, for salvation and an assurance was given me that He had taken away my sins, even mine, and saved me from the law of sin and death.

Eighteen days later, before the University of Oxford, Wesley preached his famous sermon, *"By Grace Are Ye Saved Through Faith."* That message sounded the keynote of his ministry and that doctrine became the rallying standard of the new movement he was to found—the Methodist church.

Denied the privilege of preaching in the State of England churches, Wesley took to the field, the halls, the streets, anywhere! His philosophy, "I look on the world as my parish," was memorably manifested when he used his father's tombstone for a pulpit and preached to the largest crowd ever to assemble in Epworth. *Revival broke out!* He stayed on eight more days. His sermons were drowned out by the cries of sinners seeking salvation. The last meeting lasted three hours.

Wesley's ministry widened. The crowds came—five thousand, ten, fifteen, sometimes twenty thousand. And

PROFILES IN EVANGELISM

the mobs came, too. In his *Journal*, the times that he told of attempts on his life are unbelievable, unimaginable! Stonings! Rioting! Clubbing! Draggings through the streets, etc., were commonplace when Wesley preached. His *Journal* reads like pages out of the book of Acts.

But Wesley persisted and preached. Souls were saved. Societies were organized. Preachers were assigned. Class meetings were organized. "Rules" for the societies were published. England, Ireland and Scotland were evangelized. The whole of Britain was changed, transformed under the impassioned, Christ-honoring, evangelistic preaching of Wesley and his methodical, disciplined organization efforts. And the outreach of Wesley's ministry spanned the Atlantic Ocean and spawned the largest Protestant denomination America has known.

Wesley was a unique, many-faceted man. He was an evangelist, a musician (*sometime count the hymns of Wesley in your hymnal*), a genius at organization, a scholar. In his theology, Wesley was an Arminian as contrasted with Calvinism. He was a disciplinarian and indefatigable. Slight of build (*he was five feet, five inches tall*), never weighing over one hundred and twenty pounds, was tubercular in his early life. Yet, he was a giant for God in his ministry. His travels took him over a quarter of a million miles on horseback! He preached 42,000 messages. He wrote over two hundred books. A few days before he died, at eighty-eight, he preached to sinners to get saved, *"Seek ye the Lord while he may be found."*

His sister well described him as "Out of breath, seeking souls." Doubtlessly, Wesley best described himself and his ministry when he testified, "Is not this a brand plucked out of the fire?"

George Whitefield
Evangelist
(1714-1770)

Contemporary and co-laborer with John Wesley in the great revival of the Eighteenth Century that spared England and America from the ravages of the French Revolution was George Whitefield. Doubtlessly no evangelist has ever realized the results and achieved the popularity Whitefield enjoyed in evangelism. His biography reads more like fiction, a fairy story and fantasy.

His conversion was unique. At fifteen he was a "common drawer" as he tended bar. "Much pressed" about his soul, Whitefield read the Bible while "sitting up at night." *"Seeking to work out a righteousness of his own,"* he so *"submitted himself to mortifications of his body"* that he nearly died. It was in this state as he lay on his bed, tongue parched with fever, that the words of Christ, "I thirst. I thirst," impressed his mind. Whitefield cried out to God in hope, "I thirst. I thirst for Thy pardoning love! Lord, I believe, help Thou my unbelief." His prayer was heard, for as Whitefield testified: "The load of guilt and terror and anxiety, that weighted down my spirit while I sinfully and ungratefully hesitated to trust in Divine grace, was gone."

Whitefield was saved. He soon enrolled in Oxford where he became a friend of the Wesleys and was ordained to preach, June 20, 1736.

The crowds he preached to were unparalleled in evangelism. At twenty-two he had crowds in London so "vast it was necessary to place constables both inside and outside the churches to preserve the peace." At Kingwood,

George Whitefield

George Whitefield 213

near Bristol, preaching to brutal, barbarous, violent colliers living in the deepest drunkenness and degradation, Whitefield saw the crowds swell from one hundred to twenty thousand. Whitefield called on Wesley to come and help him. At first, Wesley demurred. He was an Oxford graduate, scholarly, and cultured. Like England, he was shocked that anyone would preach to such crude people and outside the church walls. But he went. He saw Whitefield's success and he was won over. The next day he preached. "The Wesleyan Revival was on! It lasted nearly fifty years."

A scattered sampling of Whitefield's attendances: Mooreheads—1739—30,000 in attendance sometimes. Philadelphia—12,000; 22,000. Boston—"weather wet, but above 8,000 followed into the fields." "Saturday, about 15,000 people on the Common." Farewell sermon "to nearly 30,000 people, though the whole population of Boston did not at that time exceed 20,000." The list is endless. These attendances are the more remarkable in the light of the fact that those were days of infidelity, profligacy, debauchery and formalism in England and America.

His conquests and converts for Christ were probably unparalleled by any evangelist, too. Remember Kingwood? Whitefield wrote of those meetings:

"Sometimes employed almost from morning to night answering those who, in distress of soul, cried out, 'What must I do to be saved?' "

American cities were rocked with the same kind of revival! New York—"Whole congregation alarmed. Shrieking, wailing, weeping were to be heard in every corner. Men's hearts failing them for fear." "Thousands and tens of thousands gathered to Christ!" Similar sentences could be penned about Philadelphia, Boston, New England, the Southern states; England, Ireland, etc. The results read like pages out of the book of Acts. I simply summarize his soul-winning successes with this quotation

214   *PROFILES IN EVANGELISM*

of Dr. James Hamilton:

> When it is realized that his voice could be heard by twenty thousand, and that ranging all over the empire, as well as America, he would often preach thrice on a working day, and that he has received in one week as many as a thousand letters from persons awakened by his sermons, if no estimate can be formed of the results of his ministry, some idea may be suggested of its vast extent and singular effectiveness.

Which leads me to suggest the qualifications for evangelism that God gave him in unmeasured quantity. He had the vocal power for open-air and mass ministry. "It was loud and clear, and he articulated his words so that he could be understood for great distances." God gave him great physical power for his demanding ministry. He preached "in the compass of a single week, and that for thirty years, in general forty hours, and in many sixty, and that to thousands. Never, perhaps, since the apostolic age, has any man given himself so entirely to preaching the Gospel of Christ for the salvation of souls. . . ."

And God gave him great oratorical powers. Whitefield is considered a prince of English preachers, a peer of pulpit orators, eclipsing all in the "power of darting the Gospel direct into the conscience. His thoughts were possessions, and his feelings transformations, and he spoke because he felt, his hearers understood because they saw."

But Whitefield's greatest powers were his spiritual gifts and greatness. He was a man of prayer—*"Had he been less prayerful, he would have been less powerful."* He was a student of Scripture—*he once read Matthew Henry's six volumes on his knees, pausing and praying God would engraft his mind with the instructions of that extraordinary man.* He was a lover of souls—"I could willingly go to prison or to death for you, so I could but bring one soul from the Devil's strongholds, into the salvation which is in Christ Jesus." Space limits me to just some mere words that measured the man: tenderness, tears, earnestness, selflessness, humility, genuineness.

On September 30, 1770, nearly fifty-six years old, George Whitefield, who preached for thirty-four years, crossed the Atlantic thirteen times, preached more than eighteen thousand sermons, influenced one of the greatest revivals, died at Newburyport, Massachusetts, is found "suddenly exchanging his life of unparalleled labors for his eternal rest."

For a complete list of books available from the Sword of the Lord, write to Sword of the Lord Publishers, P. O. Box 1099, Murfreesboro, Tennessee 37133.

(800) 251-4100
(615) 893-6700
FAX (615) 848-6943
www.swordofthelord.com